Evil Psychologist in a Culture of Denial:
A Victim's Story of Bullying in the NHS

Story Arc & Analysis with
Suggested Preventative Measures
For investigating bully managers
& compensating victims

by

Marianne Richards MSc.
Anti Bullying at Work Campaigner

ISBN: 9798665244686

Published by InspirationWorks4U.co.uk

Cover design by Mole Graphics

BRICKS

To put one brick upon another
Add a third and then a fourth
Leaves no time to wonder whether
What you do has any worth.

But to sit with bricks around you
While the winds of heaven bawl
Weighing what you should or can do
Leaves no doubt of it at all.

Philip Larkin

DEDICATION

Dedicated to the bravery of NHS whistleblowers
striving to make workplaces safe -
and to those who genuinely support them.

CONTENTS

INTRODUCTION

I myself have experienced workplace bullying, as well as read and researched countless cases of other victims, in the NHS and elsewhere. Shockingly, bullying of staff by managers in the NHS is widespread, reported by reputable press agencies & professional journals, with verifiable sources:

- https://bmjopen.bmj.com/content/3/6/e002628
- https://www.nhsemployers.org/retention-and-staff-experience/tackling-bullying-in-the-nhs
- https://www.theguardian.com/society/2016/oct/26/nhs-staff-bullying-culture-guardian-survey

Like many victims, I protested loudly and regularly, after being bullied by my manager. This was at great personal risk. As well as substantial losses, I was humiliated, ostracised, ridiculed then punished by AWP Board, when the bully and her cronies lied to save their careers. I was;

- threatened with legal action & 'punitive costs'
- falsely accused of 'criticising the Trust' at University;
- eventually blacklisted from my profession
- financially ruined when an administrative contract was illegally terminated
- my mental health in tatters, the Head of Psychology falsely accused me of 'deliberately avoiding disciplinary procedures'
- losing my home, false accusations ringing in my ears, I attempted suicide
- I was ostracised for 'lack of language' during this extensive trauma -
  - HR staff not accounting for my PTSD;
  - misrepresenting my justified outrage 'as if' it were my usual character
- forced by circumstances to accept derisory, draconian settlement during my trauma, without sufficient legal help;
- AWP continually refused mediation, including ACAS and MP intervention, with no consequence or conscience shown by the Board
- continual blackening of my name in inter-departmental emails, repeating hearsay emanating from the bully, repeated endlessly by her sycophants
- agencies like PALS colluding (hidden social networks)
- unable to reach Tribunal because of blocking by AWP legal team
- unable to obtain closure, comprising these elements;
  1. acknowledgement of wrongdoing & putting things right
  2. apologising to me

3. offering full, fair references to allow continuation of my career
4. assistance to find suitable alternative employment
5. offering therapy OUTSIDE the organisation
6. a fair reparation (judicial settlement)

Why I Wrote This Report

'If you deconstruct something, its meaning, intentions and agendas separate and rise to the surface very quickly and everything unravels.' Information is Beautiful , David McCandless, 2009.

I originally wrote this for the Senior President of Tribunals, asking that after scrutiny it would be filed in the archives for use of researchers, journalists and scholars - anyone researching bullying-at-work, particularly in the NHS.

I wanted to speak on behalf of victims like myself; our lives ruined then cheated out of fair settlement and closure. I am a leit motif for countless victims. It is during my long recovery, almost 16 years to date, I discovered documents that proved an extensive a cover-up at Avon & Wiltshire Mental Health Trust and began to perceive the dynamics. AWP's amateur, biased 'investigations' had devastated my career, private and social life, terminating in a breakdown [psychosis] and suicide attempt. I suffer periodic PTSD to this day.   My case against the bully was never investigated:

1. documents had been withheld until it was too late for investigation;
2. my mental ill health and trauma (anger, disbelief, disempowerment) prevented my analyzing what happened and how, until years later.
3. the cover-up was cunningly conducted, by the bully & her senior colleagues who also
4. mislead investigatory bodies, with lies about non-existent investigations, abusing HR systems, abusing psychological knowledge, for example of the 'halo effect'
5. sycophants were favoured and promoted by the bully, to induce false 'corroboratory' reports;
6. evidence by whistleblowers was ignored by AWP Board, including that of their own solicitor

7. AWP paying £thousands in legal fees to Bevan Britten, notorious for preventing NHS staff from receiving apology, fair settlement and closure, through gamesmanship (abuse of knowledge of the law).
8. AWP HR & Board seemingly encouraging victimization of whistle-blowers

This analysis was impossible until recently for several reasons:
1. my recovery has been longer than expected,
2. spiralling hearsay, extending the scope & nature of hurts
3. shadows of other documents prove important evidence was withheld, destroyed or tampered with
4. I was harried by AWP legal team, threatened with 'punitive legal costs' and defamation, my credibility destroyed by repetition of vile hearsay (which all traced back to the bully)

Sixteen years on, I find the material draining and have not read every word of it. Accusatory, offensive, inter-departmental emails. Disgruntled colleagues' petty grudges, allowing gross exaggerations by bully supports. The only individuals I admire are those who came forward despite being themselves criticised by the clique. Sixteen years might seem a very long time yet is not, for someone enduring such vile emotional battering. Courts do not take account of this. **We are a silent army trudging like ghosts around Tribunals without getting in**.

I have been prevented by Beven Britten from achieving a full hearing for 16 years. This is disgraceful, immoral and unjust. In 2017, 40% of claimants at Bristol Tribunal were litigants-in-person. Discovering this to be commonplace, I became an anti bullying campaigner. I never wanted this, only to continue my career in mental health and my life as a respected author. I lost all of these things and a lot more too.

I want a fair deal for victims. I have over 1000 documents in a searchable database, revealing how easy it is for rogue employees to operate - how collusion prevents victims speaking out. If as a result of this report someone intervenes, that would be amazing. This needs changes in legislation to prevent situations arising and to take the power of investigation away from large NHS Trusts. I knowing little of the dynamics of law, but I know it does not offer victims moral justice. At the end of this report, I offer suggestions to Tribunals, genuine HR seniors &

investigatory bodies, to make outcomes fairer for victims. Hopefully, to prevent bullying and collusion - decrying it publicly as whistleblowers do, without thanks and often against hostile employers like AWP.

Urban Myths Promulgated, When Victims are Silenced

It is an urban myth that help agencies offering help to victims of toxic employers are effective. This myth is promulgated through public image and also unwittingly by Tribunal staff, including Judges. I will outline my experience of the abuse of external systems by rogue employers; the narrow nature of their remit; how lack of resources render them ineffective. I do not know if they are subject to statistics, conducted by independent bodies, but this would be a better way of measuring effectiveness.

Why Tribunal & other investigatory bodies do not work may not be apparent at high level. If victims are silenced (prevented from stating their experience and presenting evidence in court), facts will be silenced. For example, in many Tribunal applications I was passed urban myths about 'free legal help'; experienced legal professionals mislead me about admin requirements e.g. bundle content; also senior staff promulgating destruction of my reputation to render me voiceless to successive C.E.'s [secondary bullying] as well as outside investigators over-influenced by titles and 'known' staff of long standing who were not necessarily truthful.

Tribunal 'Out of Time' Rules Preventing Closure for Victims

Metaphor: unlike the police, Tribunals do not employ forensic staff to investigate post tribunal evidence, for example when documents have been deliberately withheld. The police hold evidence on file in case further evidence, or victims of the same miscreant, come forward in later years. Tribunals do not carry out such practice. This holds whether evidence is personal or via documents 'disappeared' - the proverbial, 'filing bin'. Whereas victims of crime may eventually find justice and closure, very often victims of civil crimes do not.

Civil law is abused by legal professionals who have to 'win' at any cost in order to generate new clients. Thus, despite Barristers being advised to put justice above client loyalty, and explain legal technicalities to naive claimants,

16

this does not happen in practice. That is why I, for example, was disabled from presenting evidence hidden by staff or legal representatives, until too late to present to Tribunal. I believe this is termed gamesmanship.

Class Differentials, Misunderstandings & Assumptions

There are damaging assumptions by middle or upper class professionals about the behaviour of working class victims. The same applies to disabilities such as autism. These features are easily manipulated to denigrate victims, for example in presenting negative behaviours as 'malicious' when they arise as reactions to extreme stress e.g. bullying. These circumstances are likely to be hidden from Court - misrepresentation by employer legal professionals; lack of knowledge about hidden disability and social mores. This is further promulgated by rendering victims voiceless, before, during or after stressful court procedures AND because court procedures are unfathomable to the victims who have no legal help – which is most of them.

My Qualifications/Disability Relevant to this Report

'By three methods we may learn wisdom: First, by reflection, which is noblest; Second, by imitation, which is easiest; and third by experience, which is the bitterest.' Confucius

I am 67, a Counsellor in Brief Therapy with MSc. in Mental Health Practice [*among other qualifications*]. I am a professional author. I have no family. I retired age 63 after 7 years at B&Q, a poor ending through being bullied out of my profession at Avon & Wiltshire Mental Health Trust [AWP].

I have high functioning autism, Asperger Syndrome [1: Docs A & A1 to A8a]; a complex disability often misrepresented by the employer i.e. head of Psychology, Dr William Jerrom, falsely stated Asperger Syndrome = inability to empathise [2: Doc B, p4 para 8], disputing a Tribunal decision [3] that I had a disability at the time of my Tribunal. I was diagnosed in 2009 during treatment for depression, itself the result of bullying at AWP. Autism is a sensory disorder with marked difficulties in communication i.e. neurotypicals perceive the world differently; thus we lead stressful lives, divided by language.

When stressed, I have huge difficulty communicating: get over-detailed, jump subjects, take hours / days to write what usually takes an hour or two, become disheartened, stressed or depressed. Dr Jerrom's view of autism though claiming expertise, is not up to date, in parts incorrect or downright untruthful [experts listed in Cast of Characters].

metaphor: "*The Etruscan inscriptions are written in Greek letters and can therefore be read, but the language is not understood.*" Derek Roe, Prehistory.

I was disabled from presenting evidence at Tribunal for THIRTEEN YEARS by AWP legal team. I developed PTSD and Diabetes 2 as a result. I still suffer PTSD, lost teeth to night grinding, have black days with suicidal thoughts. What keeps me going is campaigning - offering victims a voice via my website.

I hope this report of my experience, including documentary evidence, helps Tribunals understand the dynamics from a victim's point of view. I hope this leads to beneficial change. I do not know if it is too late for me to be helped to a fairer resolution, but that is not the issue.

My story shows my suffering, that of other victims ignored by AWP and of the many THOUSANDS of other victims who have been silenced. My analysis shows my intellect and what my former employer lost, in preventing my career in adult mental health - for no just cause. My analysis has become my life work; a role as an anti bullying campaigner foist on me by circumstances. Nevertheless, I will carry it well and for as long as it takes to make changes - as once I carried out my professional duties at AWP.

I do not seek apology from the miscreants – that too is now irrelevant – but I want those who have the power to change things to know why, and how, these things happen, and what to do about it - effectively.

MY EMPLOYMENT WITH AWP

'Agenda for Change' [A4C] - Backcloth

Agenda for Change was imposed on the NHS by the Government, considerably changing training and working conditions for adult mental health staff. No extra funding was provided and there was huge opposition by traditionalist staff. The new dynamics triggered arguments about conditions, hours & pay, setting staff as rivals. Newly-qualified psychologists feared their degrees would be downgraded, through 'unqualified' mental health workers from complementary medicine being given jobs on their pay scales, with the same opportunity of advancement. There was considerable hostility toward Complementary practitioners that does not exist now.

I was a mental health worker recruited under this scheme, offered free Masters Degree training and a mentor, though the latter never materialised.

The department I joined was heavily under A4C stressors but I was not informed before signing the contract. I learned this much later. Neither did Dignity at Work 'investigators' put these facts in their report. They ought to have done, as this had considerable bearing on departmental stress for which I was later victimised.

My Life Before Avon & Wiltshire Mental Health Trust [AWP]

Before I entered AWP I had a fat file of testimonials: employers [4: Doc C], associates, publisher and private patients. I had a Victorian cottage and garden I restored over 5 years, professional network, friends of similar vision, an author of repute:

[5: see website
https://www.amazon.co.uk/Marianne-Richards/e/B0034NZAKK%3Fref=dbs_a _mng_rwt_scns_share].

Bullying At Eldene Surgery, Swindon

I began working for AWP in 2004 as a part time Counsellor at Eldene Surgery, Swindon. Psychologist Dr Elizabeth Howells managed the Department of

Psychology, Victoria Hospital, supplying clinical staff for Eldene. She set up the service alongside Eldene's lead GP, Dr Holliday, under A4C.   Howells had been a lab technician but now had a managerial role which (*she revealed in a rare moment*) she did not want.   She was not a people person. Eldene Practice Manager Mrs Christine Mott vociferously opposed counselling [26: Doc W, p3 8b]; two counsellors walked out because of her attitude before I took up post. Howells had not dealt with this [15: Doc L1, para 1 & 19: Doc P], neither had Training Officer, Annette Law or Counsellor Cluster Lead, Barbara Stapleton. I was informed by a District Nurse of regular, petty bullying of staff under Mrs Mott's regime. I believe this was partly due to Dr Holliday failing to address financial and administrative problems, to the frustration of Mrs Mott. She took this out on staff. I was expected to counsel patients under these conditions;

- vociferous opposition and insults by Mott about counselling, in front of admin staff;
- 'jokes' about suicide [*on the wall of the counselling room; a postcard of a cliff directly beneath one of a cemetery];*
- *broken chairs for counsellor and patient to sit on, full sharps boxes and overflowing bins*
- *making appointments whilst I was on leave then claiming I had deliberately missed them*
- *that my 'did not attends' were too high, when appointments and computer entries had been altered by Mott.*
- *a patient suicide note left unattended in my tray, whilst I was on leave* [*19: Doc P, p2 no 9]*

Bullying at Victoria Hospital

I worked in the office one day at week whilst at Eldene Surgery. I worked there six months before being offered another part time post at Victoria Hospital, on the psychology assistant pay scales. This brought me up to full time. Howells' Secretary Veronica Barnes had chronic back pain and was often abrupt. As soon as I went into the office, once a week, I would be challenged over trivia, e.g. why I asked for two stamps to send in returns. She would then telephone Howells at night, crying down the telephone and criticising me. This fired up Howells, who made confusing, contradictory directions [21: Doc R3 & Doc R4].

Much stress was down to Howells' difficulty with staff; errors of judgement, unable to cope with challenges, getting exasperated. A lot of this came my way [15, Doc L2]. Psychology Assistants would complain to Barnes as they dare not approach Howells, knowing   Barnes was supported by Howells in return for 'information' on staff. Howells would shout at staff, set them spying on each other. She gave complex directions for working out overtime pay, offered unworkable 'choices' [15: Doc L4]that would frustrate admin staff. My impression was of Howells putting staff in distress and confusion, taking attention from her incapability of processing A4C whilst portraying her as a 'good' Manager.

Howells began asking me to attend weekly 'line management' meetings; an arrangement no one else had. She garnered personal information during these meetings, information of a very personal kind I did not want to share. After a week or two, she began telling me I was, 'in trouble with HR' but without substantiating this. As I have autism, it did not occur me to question this, but I was very worried. She said she would, 'protect me' but in return I had to tell her, 'what goes on in the office'. During later meetings, she homed in on topics she knew I found upsetting, for example isolation in my family. I knew nothing of autism, being undiagnosed, but later discovered my brother and father had been thus afflicted, making ours an 'odd' family (in the 1950's). I began to come out these meetings in tears. This happened so often Training Manager Annette Law informed HR I was, 'over emotional'. New to the NHS, fearing I would lose my post, I would be on edge until Howells breezed in, often weeks later, staring and smiling at me, greeting me as if nothing had happened. She repeated this several times before I realized I was being emotionally abused.

In 2004, Howells cancelled my part time post at the Victoria at short notice after indicating at the start that it would continue. Though HR Manager Andrew Mitchell claimed this was the natural end of contract [6: Doc E2 & 24: Doc U1] this was untrue. At the time I had been applying to Sarsen Housing for a key worker housing grant which HR knew about [6: Doc E7]. HR and Howells knew I was visiting suitable properties and I would not have done so if I had prior knowledge of the contract being time limited. This was not the only time Howells cancelled contracts at short notice - another control method. She gave staff very small contracts, setting them vying with each other for extra hours. These were first indications of sadism in her personality.

I gave Howells a list of concerns about Eldene affecting patient care, it having already been acknowledge this was a 'problem' Surgery [19: Doc P & 15: Doc L1]. Disclosures years later revealed my list annotated in her handwriting, 'time for a new counsellor?' [19: Doc P]. In 2005, exhausted by Practice Manager Christine Mott's childish behaviours, also Howells' lack of support, both of them effectively sabotaging my efforts to counsel patients, I complained to HR.

HR Refuse Investigation
HR Manager Andrew Mitchell shockingly told me, 'I am not going to anything. She is our best manager'. I remember his exact words. When Howells found out she began nit-picking [15: Docs L1 & Doc L2], which was suspiciously weeks after providing an over-egged, almost sarcastic testimonial [15: Doc L1]. It was also at odds with her remarks to HR [24: Doc U1, p3 point7] As I proved each lie untrue, she found new faults. Rather than suspicion at the catalogue of accusations, Mitchell said, 'she made so many complaints, some must be true' [undisclosed in 2017 but disclosed in 2006]. He appeared exasperated.

Seeking Help from Staff Health & Head of Psychology
As relations with Howells deteriorated, I lost confidence. I approached Staff Health. Dr Ochoa asked her to moderate her behaviour [17: Doc N1 & Doc N2]. Howells began a series of complaints to Occupational Health, about myself and other staff appointments. Her 'concerns' about me were mis-representations of my mental health; false claims about my talking about

presumed mental problems in work time [17: Doc N4], referring to 'psychotic episodes' - I had ONE psychosis after a breast operation went wrong in June 2000 {17: Doc N6]i.e. three years before my employ. I was made to attend Staff health three times [24: Doc U1, p2 no 4]. Much later during searches for Tribunal disclosure, I discovered extensive, unauthorised interference in my medical records and attempts to speak to the Counsellor my GP provided:

1. GP medical records in a mess when I went to peruse them at Westbury Surgery- the years mixed up
2. Howells asked Dr Holliday to approach my GP Counsellor, Caroline Wiltshire [24: U1, p2 point 5]
3. in AWP disclosures, confidential notes from Green Lane hospital I had never seen [24: Doc U3 & Doc U3a]
4. on the 23 Jan 2004 a 'Brenda Moore' telling Westbury Surgery she was a 'Psychiatrist' 'working in my department as a Psychologist', claiming I was 'behaving erratically. paranoid and aggressive'[17: Doc N5] - no documentation was disclosed by AWP on this. The only 'Moore' was HR Manager, Abigail Moore. I have never heard of Brenda Moore - she does not appear on the email staff list compiled for e-newsletters.
5. in the same document [17: Doc N5] in July 2005, my GP noted Howells phoning me at home, using my mental health as an excuse and becoming aggressive over the phone

My gut feeling is, Howells was attempting to pass off my workplace stress as pre-existing mental disorder, to avoid investigation of her bullying. nb GP Index records [17: Doc N5 & Doc N6] prove I was highly distressed in 2004 by Howells behaviour and not, as she reframed it, because I was unstable [26: Doc W, p4 point 12].

When Howells did not desist, I approached Head of Psychology, Dr William Jerrom, suggesting mediation. He said I could withdraw this complaint or he would set up a Dignity investigation. As his investigation began, I was signed off again with stress - the first of many until I walked out on GP advice. This is well documented in my medical notes, which Bevans attempted to keep out of the bundle.

I recently discovered how Howells had spread misinformation to Mitchell and Jerrom [21: Doc R6] seeding the idea I had been 'refusing management,' not

23

attending supervision and training, and exaggerating colleague disputes, which were widespread in this dysfunctional department. My autism certainly was a part of this mix, but not to the extent of singling me out for extensive, harrowing disciplinary actions injurious to my career, with so many seniors joining the attack. And during this, I was expected to counsel mentally ill patients living in a socially deprived area, with Mott's constant criticism, and sabotaging the service where she could.

Notable about Howells' behaviour were factitious claims about my work and personality as a lever to institute, 'performance management', claiming she had been 'attempting' this 'going on two years' [26: Doc W, p1 no 3a]. Instead of checking the veracity of her many complaints Mitchell colluded, by again misrepresenting the Union meeting then writing of 'measures' they had decided upon [21: Doc R5]. If this documental 'evidence' by a Personal Officer was later seen by senior HR or the Board, I understand how easy it would be to assume that I had been behaving badly, when I had not, particularly if they were lazy and did not read all the documents. (I assume this is why much had been withheld or 'disappeared').

This negative presentation of me was at odds with other documental evidence. An email she sent on 2 June 2005, 'you do indeed work very hard.' [15: Doc L5] The only appraisal disclosed by AWP is dated July 2004 [15: Doc L1a] - and not indicative of a dissolute employee. This includes a list of CPD training I had completed. There was also my supervision diary which Law had seen many times, as I took it to every supervision session. Howells University testimonial [15: Doc L1] also gives the lie to her complaints. In conclusion, this behaviour is indicative of a sadistic personality, which I and Helen agreed pointed to sociopathic personality order. It is shocking her highly experience psychology colleagues did not spot the signs, particularly when Howells escalated to, '[Marianne] threatened staff with physical violence.' Annette Law would definitely have acted upon this and Barnes or Stapleton would certainly have reported it, as would members of staff and senior Counsellors.

There was no way the Dignity at Work could be impartial, investigators being seeded with highly damaging untruths, disciplinary procedures implemented on the basis of specious arguments put forward by Howells and repeated verbatim by Booth, Jerrom and Stancliffe, with no one in senior HR checking their veracity. This is why I was so angry, insisting they investigate further - which never happened.

Performance Management - Based on Sophistry

Soon after Dr Ochoa's letter, Howells had instigated a 'Performance Management' based on her lies about my work, which were either believed or glossed over by HR. Both the original allegations and Performance management were never again checked, but 'accepted' as true.

AWP solicitor, Rahim Amarshi, wrote to Andrew Mitchell querying 7 accusations in this 'performance management' he discovered to be without foundation [21: Doc R1, p4 points 1-7]**. Amarshi's objections went ignored, though Howells' trumped-up accusations / performance management were the basis of further HR processes including a Dignity at Work and suspension during my absence with depressive illness [17: Doc N6].

IMPORTANT NOTE
** During my final appeal to His Honour, Mr Justice Swift, I felt he misunderstood my reason for pointing out Amarshi's letter to Andrew Mitchell. Mr Justice Swift said it was Amarshi's job was to act Devil's Advocate over evidence - WHEREAS I wanted to show the Judge this was concrete evidence I had been bullied and others had been bullied too; a fact denied by Booth, Jerrom & Mitchell as part of their cover-up. I wanted to prove I had been subjected to draconian HR processes despite my disability; a disability AWP continually denied despite extensive medical evidence. And I had been prevented from showing that medical evidence to Judge Sara in 2007 and all ensuing Tribunals; 2009, 2017 and 2018, as well as my letters of appeal.
Howells false claims were at odds with a testimonial provided in May 2005 [15: Doc L1]. This was followed on 23 June by a highly charged complaint

where she writes, 'I am writing officially once again' [15: Doc L2]- despite this being her first letter i.e. deliberate misrepresentation. This was followed by a further letter dated 23 June [21: Doc R2]. Her erratic behaviour is demonstrated by complaints of varying seriousness:

- 10 May 2004 instructing me to obtain stamps via her Secretary [21: Doc R3]
- on 20 October 2005 admonishing me for doing so [21: Doc R4].
- 'MR spent hours in core time talking to team members.. about the abuse she had suffered as a child [26: Doc W p3, point 10a]. My father NEVER abused me; ergo, I did not use work time talking of such
- '[Marianne's]work was not good' ; contrast with 15: Doc L1]
- 'had a huge personal debt' [26: W p4 point 15a] and 'borrowing money off staff.. Though this was always repaid' [26: W p515b]. I was not in debt, though sold my home fearing debt. I never borrowed off staff - ergo, the second half of her sentence is a misrepresentation or specious argument.

Misrepresentation of Union Meeting

I organised a meeting with Unison to discuss my being bullied by Howells. This was regularly misrepresented by Howells, Booth and Mitchell as a 'performance management ' meeting [20: Doc Q2, p1 para 3 'in Jul' & p2]. Mitchell denied receiving a complaint from me [20: Doc Q2, p2 para 5 'in the ET form..']. This is untenable as I disclosed to AWP a copy of my email to Unison representative, Jim D'Avila (at 19:34 on the evening of 20 June 2005), which contains a copy of my original request to Mitchell for this meeting, together with the email's auto receipt- this auto receipt proved my email to Mitchell was opened 20 June 2005 at 9:30am [20: Doc Q1 - see after red text, halfway down the page]. D'Avila replied the same day, asking if I was waiting for a response to my request [20: Doc Q3]. I emailed details to Howells on 28 June, which she forwarded to Mitchell the same day [20: Doc Q5]. I also have an email Booth sent to Jerrom [20: Q6] reiterating the misrepresentation.

In an email of 15 July 2005, Mitchell again misrepresents this as a 'meeting to discuss Howells' [falsified] performance management' [20: Q4 p1 para 3, 'in

July 2005'], re-stating claims proven untrue by Amarshi [25: Doc V, p4 -5 numbered 1 - 7]. Jerrom does exactly the same in attempting to mislead Amarshi about the same meeting [8: Doc B p2, penultimate para, text emboldened by Amarshi, 'note for BB']. During my later complaint to HPC, Stancliffe does the same [20: Q7, p2, para 2].

Escalation of Fictitious Complaints

I continually resisted the falsified procedures. This resulted in Jerrom describing me as, 'uncooperative, rude' and, 'aggressive refusal to accept reasonable management requests' with other denigrations. Tacit belief of lies told by Howells and spread as hearsay by Dr Anne Booth [her Manager and a Dignity investigator], Dr William Jerrom [head of Psychology] and Andrew Mitchell (AWP HR Manager), none of whom demanded details or evidence from Howells, allowed the hearsay to spread up the chain of command as if true. Not one of the four CE's I later approached questioned this or investigated from the ground up (my MP was informed they had).

Howells escalated with an enfilade of allegations. As I proved each untrue, the 'complaint' disappeared from HR records and another take its place. The 'disappearances' are impossible to prove, except through the negative attitude to me by HR beginning with Andrew Mitchell. In disclosures none of the early complaints appeared.

Howells made several casuist statements to HR, e.g. describing how 'nice' staff were [26: Doc W, p3 point 10a] and she was puzzled at my complaints. It appears HR were deceived by masking the in-fighting and suspicion which I experienced as a reaction to Agenda for Change (A4C) but was occurring before my employ [17: Doc N3].

Howells' sycophants were promoted and given favours in return for support. Veronica Barnes (her Secretary) and Barbara Stapleton (Cluster Lead) were not competent. Both would ring Howells at night in tears, blaming me for things that went wrong; examples are Barnes' health and safety blunders and Stapleton's University failures. The morning after such outbursts Howells would approach me angrily, sometimes shouting, sometimes in the car park before I reached the office, but never waiting for my response.

False Claims of Racism

Another example was when I took issue with vociferous Senior Assistant, Anita Corfe, who demanded details of my personal life and relationships. I told her when she was angered she reminded me of an Irish nurse who bullied me in another Trust. Corfe forced me into a room with colleague Becky Watkins, insisting Becky wrote down I had made a, 'racial comment.' This was repeated in a Dignity witness statement by Barnes, claiming I made 'racist remarks,' before trying to rescind this via Christopher Stancliffe (HR Director and Dignity investigator) [22: Doc S1]. Jerrom repeated to Amarshi that I made, 'two racist remarks' [8: B p3, para 6] # but never rescinded this.

the second was based on an incident where I was teaching with Aleya Begum, discussing equality during a stress management course. I was pointing out differences between Begum and myself; my pink skin, hers being brown; I tall and overweight, she slight in stature. This was to demonstrate the absurdity of arbitrary differences as basis for prejudice and Begum knew this, being more familiar with this teaching material. Begum made no complaint to me or I would have apologised. At worst, this might be considered a clumsy remark but it was not racial or racist. Begum was a qualified Psychology Assistant, not a newcomer.

False Claims Escalate to Criminal Allegations

I did not discover until 2017 - 2018 the following further complaints lodged against me:

1. I, 'threatened staff with physical violence [3: Doc J1 & Doc J2],
2. 'aggressive or abusive comments to colleagues including two incidents of racist comments' [8: p3 para 6],
3. 'aggressively refused management [8 para 6] - i.e. my objection to the falsified 'performance management'
4. 'bullied' Barbara Stapleton [8 p3, para 5] (*Howells subordinate, my Cluster Lead and fellow student*)
5. 'bullied everyone at AWP.'

In 2018, I was shocked to discover Howells claimed to Stancliffe that I, 'bullied everyone at AwP and 'threatened staff with physical violence' [3: Doc J1 & Doc J2 p1 point 8].   No one seemed to see anomalies between her over-blown testimonial for my Degree course[15: Doc L1] before she began claiming I bullied her [15: L2], a claim she also made to Jerrom [15: Doc L3] then later denied. Mitchell repeats this to Amarshi, claiming there was 'no evidence' of Howells bullying me but there was counter-wise [Doc Q2, p2 para 2]. Although they agreed there were no issues with my clinical work [4: Doc C & Doc C1], there was no suspicion that Howells was the only person making allegations about my 'threatening' her and others, an allegation she made to Jerrom [25: Doc V1] after I made my formal complaint and during the time he was setting up his 'Dignity at Work' investigation. I only discovered   the wicked and widely spread hearsay about 'threats' and 'violence' during 2018, when I approached FO1 for non disclosed documents in 2018, when Helen sent her testimony. It was a huge shock, explaining the continuous, very hostile, stance of AWP Board.

Leading Up To Dignity Investigation

2006 Jerrom Meeting

I went to Dr William Jerrom, Head of Psychology, complaining about Howells' behaviour. I informed him Counsellor Ingrid Schulz (member of BACP, a Training Counsellor of repute) initially diagnosed me with Asperger Syndrome whilst treating me for work-related stress. Jerrom was shocked, repeating, 'Asperger Syndrome!' whilst staring into the middle distance.   Throughout my debacle with AWP and Tribunal, Jerrom denied my autism when speaking to Rahim Amarshi prior to my Tribunal [1: doc B], misleading Amarshi about symptoms of autism [video 1: autism expert]. Though well documented, AWP legal team helped suppress my medical history, which proved workplace bullying leading to several episodes of anxiety and depression - as below. Also documented is my diagnosis of diabetes mellitus in 2015, 10 years after being bullied out of AWP (Diabetes 2 is well researched as a resultant of stress with a 10 year incubation).

Examples of medical history, as disclosed to AWP, repeated on HR files [1: Doc A to Doc A8a]

Doc A	Dr van Driel, Consultant Psychiatrist, The Bridge, Wells
Doc A1	Dr Perry, GP, Westbury Surgery
Doc A2	collage of emails re. Ingrid Schulz, Counsellor
Doc A3	Marianne to Amarshi, 29 Mar 2007, detailing how she experiences Aspergers # and what triggers her depression.
Doc A4	2017 Dr Woodward letter re mental incapacity in 2007 and 2009
Doc A5	2009 CMHT regarding Marianne at risk of suicide also [7: Doc F]
Doc A6	Many referrals for psychotherapy, i.e. PTSD, paid out of special funding
Doc A7	21 May 2015 diabetes mellitus diagnosed. Diabetes connected to stress with 10 year onset, according to research
Doc A7a	ALSO A7a: 23 Mar 2007, extract from GP index 1 of 3, p4; high weight noted Cf normal weight on peer student video, Uni of Bath
Doc A8 Doc A8a	Dr Wernham to Andrea Morland asking special funding for psychotherapy BANES commissioners / PALS - letters agreeing special funding

 # AWP made much of my stating that my Aspergers was, 'mild', trying to put out I was not troubled in daily life. Anyone experienced in autism would know this untrue. The word 'mild' was my misunderstanding when first diagnosed: I was informed Asperger Syndrome (AS or High Functioning Autism, is at the <u>mild end</u> of the spectrum - i.e., from classic to high functioning autism. This does not mean it is LESS or NOT injurious to daily life.

In classic autism patients are unable to speak or elect to do so. There might additionally be a learning disability, dyslexia or ADHD. Asperger or high functioning autism is associated with high intellect but communicating remains very difficult. That is why I ALWAYS offered colleagues mediation if there had been a communication mismatch. Jerrom interpreted autism in a way injurious and prejudicial and not up to date with knowledge even in 2006. What he claimed in the Attendance Note would horrify an autism expert. AS sufferers are known to be hyper sensitive to emotions, other people's problems and injustice.

I asked mediation but Jerrom claimed this was not possible and I must withdraw or he would set up a Dignity At Work investigation. I was hesitant, knowing Howells would react badly but I could not withdraw as what I told him was true. As soon as she found out, Howells began a systematic attack on my work, personality and behaviour.

DIGNITY AT WORK' INVESTIGATION

Jerrom Orders Dignity Investigation

Jerrom, like HR Manager Gwyneth Knight, refused my requests for mediation [25: Doc V1, para 2], claiming either Howells refused or it was 'inappropriate'. During 2017 disclosures I discovered Jerrom appointed Debbie Spaull, with HR Officer, Christopher Stancliffe, conducting interviews.

Harassment: Howells Tries to Contact GP Counsellor

I received telephone calls and a letter from Stancliffe pressing me to interview [10: G1 p1 - 2 & G2 fragment as disclosed]. I was already in anxiety and shortly after signed off [10: Doc G3 & G4 & G5 Stancliffe had been directed by Jerrom to conclude within 6 weeks.

On 13 March 2006, during my sick leave, Stancliffe sent me a letter with AWP's definition of bullying asking for a written statement [23: Doc T2]. Screen prints from Westbury surgery [*all that is left of my medical records but verifiable*] show my absences from November 2005 through March 2006, including a call from my counsellor, Caroline Wiltshire, around the time he sent this letter.

There is a reference on 13 November 2005 of Howells attempting to access Ms Wiltshire (CLW) by telephone the previous year [23: Doc T3, p3].

Stancliffe's Behaviour

Stancliffe began portraying himself as victim with HR Manager Andrew Michell's encouragement [10: Doc G6 & Doc G7]. Stancliffe persuaded Howells to make the counter claim that I had bullied her [10: Doc G8 p1 point 2b] though Howells had tried to backtrack, claiming I was 'disturbed [10: Doc G8 p1 point 2a ALSO referenced as doc W p21 point 2a]. Yet on 13th February 2006 Jerrom wrote to me of her counter claim.

To prove I was not the person Howells, and Stancliffe, were presenting, I sent Jerrom a fat file of testimonials from former and past employers, colleagues, patients and clients but he dismissed these, telling HR these were, 'irrelevant.' Likewise he ignored a peer student video which disproved Howells ' implied claim that I was not intellectually capable [video 2: Marianne's peer student presentation]. Believing hearsay, vague and contradictory complaints, indignation over things that never happened, e.g. 'racist comments' or my supposed, 'toying' with him [10: Doc G6 & Doc G7] were hallmarks of Stancliffe. He also provided a 'witness' statement for the Dignity investigation, making outrageous claims despite not having met me, read my medical history or interviewed me [31: Doc Y3].

I am not sure what triggered Judge Livesey's anger during the 2017 Tribunal [refer 30: Trib 10b & Trib 10c] about Stancliffe, but Judge Livesey angrily repeated Stancliffe's name before praising me. This was witnessed by AWP Barrister, Ms Anya Palmer. The Dignity witness reports demonstrate lack of professionalism in interviewing also bias, allowing 'witnesses' to make vague allegations without details or evidence and repeating office gossip. These allegations subsequently passed from Stancliffe, in writing, to Booth and Jerrom, thence up the hierarchy, each layer never checking the veracity but relying on the senior staff being truthful.

Mitchell's Witness Statement

Around March 2007 Mitchell took, 'management of [Marianne's] overall case' [23: Doc T4] yet in disclosures there is no report, documents or correspondence discussing findings. After our only meeting, I sent Mitchell, 'Bully Insight ' by Tim Field, world expert on bullying at work. I thought Mitchell had no notion of the dynamics of bullying - for example, telling me Howells was, 'our best Manager' in the face of counter evidence and refusing to deal with my compliant in 2006, claiming he did not receive my request for a meeting. I occasionally send books to people, including my MP. I was hoping this would help Mitchell understand links between stress and bullying and how it is commonplace for staff to substantially change character under duress. Mitchell began describing me in highly negative, distressing terms, e.g. 'condescending' [31: Doc Y1, p1, point 2bi], 'making threats' [31: Doc Y1, p2 point 2b v], 'making veiled threats' [31: Doc Y1, p2 point 2b iv] and 'she sees herself as an expert' [31: Doc Y1, p4, point 4b iv].

Although Amarshi wrote to Mitchell, confirming Millar's statement and there was evidence manager bullying [25: Doc V, p4 - 5 numbers 1-7] no correspondence following this was disclosed to or from Mitchell. Mitchell later became a Director, HR Expert.

The following document reiterates false information; the supposed Disciplinary which was in reality a meeting I organised with Unison to discuss Howells behaviour to me. It also, repeated Dr Howells had 'never made an allegation of bullying' [cf 20: Doc Q4 p2, 'ET claim point 5' no 1] and claiming HR Officer, Gwyneth Knight, suggested mediation with Howells (which had been my suggestion to Jerrom).

Howells 'Witness Statement'[all from 26: Doc W]
As with other 'statements' this contains contradictions
- p2, point 3a that Howells felt, 'extremely threatened and frightened' by me - not recorded elsewhere
- p2, point 4, 4b claiming the WCC reference was 'poor' -
  - cf Wiltshire county Council reference[26: Doc W1] (which was in AWP disclosures)
  - cf further testimonials - before and after employ with Dr Howells
      Doc W9: 2010 B&Q Manager customer service testimonial
      Doc W10: 2011 B&Q Manager Testimonial
      Doc W11: 1994 Salvation Army Testimonial   [re. Miriam: I changed by Deed Poll to Marianne]
- p1, point 2: describing me as, 'disturbed' therefore I 'could not' have bullied her
- p1, para 2b Stancliffe claiming, 'a manager could be bullied by a subordinate'
- p1, 3a Howells 'felt extremely threatened and frightened.. trying to placate [myself] over 2 years'
- p15 point 37a, 3rd bullet point: 'MR has bullied the whole of AWP'
- p 15 para 37a bullet 3: 'I was advised to instigate performance management' - Howells originated this

- p6 point 19d 'another example was the database..unprompted and without consultation she fouled the whole system necessitating its re-writing over three or four days'
  - [cf Doc V p6, para 1]Amarshi to Mitchell 'I've received an email from the Claimant in relation to a database which she says she created and which she says she has passed to various people in the Trust.' i.e. asking the return of my database; an inventory of charities and services in the county.
- p6, point 21a: 'MR accused LH of shouting at her.. MR later explained that she may have misinterpreted LH because her father would shout at her when angry and LH appeared angry'. [*my father was classically autistic - rarely spoke. When angry, he would sit in silence*]
- p7, point 22b 'MR sent emails to Assistants at a later date asking for help which upset them a lot but they felt unable to work with her"
  - refer [26: Doc W2] - Marianne's letter to all staff on day of walking out of AWP
- p7, point 23a - b; re-framing Marianne's request for mediation with Anita Corfe:
  - refer [26: Doc W3] Annette Law re Marianne and Anita]
  - also refer [26: Doc W4] O. Health Dr Salmon re Marianne's penchant for self disclosure
  - also refer [26: Doc W5] Annette Law's insightful supervision reference
- p10, point 34b - d, Howells' paranoia ('does not know if this is a rational fear') and lack of confidence; shocking terms to describe Marianne -
  - 'nasty emails',
  - 'threatening and abusive emails', #
  - 'threat', 'abusive',
  - '[Howells] hasn't hitherto felt physically threatened,'
  - 'service has been brought to its knees as a result of a lack of confidence in herself [i.e. Howells] and in AWP'
  - '[Howells] does not understand why she cannot cope with this.'
- p11, bullet 3 - 6 'MR sent a threatening email on 23rd December' #
  - [refer 26: Doc W6 & W7 & W8] letters to /from Knight; 23/12/2005 #
- p12, point 35b '[MR] would always leave submitting statistics.. seemed to take pleasure in this'

- stats included our monthly expense forms. Accounts confirmed mine were always on time

'threatening' 1st used by Knight [26: Doc W8, 23 to 28 Dec 2005]

Stapleton's Witness Statement [22: Doc S4]

Mentors were offered with the post but despite my asking many times Mitchell failed to provide one. Later he claimed Stapleton was my mentor and the rules had changed. At University Stapleton never spoke to me, spending all her breaks in the senior common room. I spent mine in the library, grounds or in the classroom with other students where we had a kettle. I am autistic and prefer my own company. The course was once a week and I spent considerable time wondering why she was ignoring me.

It was not until over a year after I left that I discovered what had gone on. Stapleton told Booth she felt, 'sick to the stomach' seeing me, claiming I bullied her [22: Doc S2] and other staff.   Stapleton did not tell Booth I taught her to use computers, she having no experience whilst I passed ECDL [European Computer Driving Licence] and designed my own website. I was confident with peers and researchers. Whilst my early assignments were of merit level, my marks dropped off [22: Doc S3] as Stapleton joined Howells in castigating me, instead of performing her role as my mentor and cluster lead. My Degree Supervisor would confirm I was studying hard and 'on track' for Distinction or Merit. I studied mental health 20 years in three NHS Trusts, in private healthcare and plus home study. That is why my career is such a loss to me.

When I challenged Stapleton's claim, HR claimed I, 'threatened her with Court,' 'marked her low' on an assignment and, 'criticised the Trust' in class. I am sure the latter was her misinterpreting a research paper I presented (advocating US health be run by groups lead by clinical staff) [34: ZZ7a & ZZ7b]; this is now being advocated for the NHS . Stapleton told Dignity investigator Anne Booth I sent a, 'vitriolic email'. I no longer have the two emails but AWP disclosed these as document numbers 4L, p5 & 7. The content was innocent, asking why she was ignoring me, reminding her as a professional mediator she must surely agree to mediation.   There was no

37

response but disclosures show she forwarded these to Howells with the cryptic message, 'and so it goes on' - disclosed by AWP as document number 4L p5 18 July 2005. Stapleton told Howells she, 'would have done better if [I] had not bullied her '[22: Doc S2]; a claim she made to my tutor, Mrs Boldison, causing a rift. Stapleton was confused by debating. She was a traditionalist, perceiving new ideas as subversive - ignoring research probably accounts for her low marks which she claimed were because I bullied her.

Agenda for Change engendered substantive changes to the way therapy was conducted, 'stepped care' being based on Brief Therapy, itself derived from complementary medicine. I had used a similar method in private healthcare but Stapleton and other traditionalists wanted things as they were. I was comfortable at University [video 2 Uni & video 2b post-Uni] but Stapleton seemed out of her depth; confused, never challenging peers in debates or presenting new research or putting forward academic arguments. Instead, she blamed her lack of success and stress on fictitious bullying, by me.

Pattern: Seniors Disabling Complaints, Repeating Hearsay

Stapleton informed our class her son had re-written an essay for her as he felt it incompetent ('you can't send that in, mum' - verbatim by Stapleton).   This was twisted by Howells during the Dignity investigation, claiming she 'had to re-write' my essays - implying I was cheating but thereby implying she had done this for other staff. Fearing my Degree being invalidated, I complained to British Psychological Society, with 'permission' from AWP. Booth and Jerrom wrote to BPS repeating the same hearsay such that BPS, after initial correspondence, failed to reply - so I gave up.

Intervention in a formal complaint became a pattern. I wrote to Health Professionals Council about Jerrom and Booth passing Howells' untruthful image of me. As hearsay spread, it was becoming impossible to contain it or discover the originators of accusations.

I could not have produced this report until this year. Even now, re-reading their shocking allegations, it is hard to bear the emotional

pain. I was unaware until late disclosures (2017) Stancliffe had written to HPC [24: U5]:

1. attaching 'one investigation report' - no details given; attachment not disclosed
2. sinister implication of consequences- if they were 'legally obliged' to reveal documents to me
3. repeating my claims were 'unjustified' - ignoring Amarshi's findings [21: R1 p4] #
4. claiming it would be too psychologically damaging to the staff involved [ignoring my trauma]
5. repeating falsifications of the Unison meeting [20: Docs Q1 to Q7]
6. reiterating the trumped-up performance management #
7. repeating I, 'refused to participate' in the Dignity investigations [23: Doc T3 medical evidence of depression]
8. writing of the 'disciplinary' # [21: R7 Stancliffe to Marianne 'you have bullied and harassed your line manager and colleagues']
9. alleging my 'disparaging the Trust' - i.e. Stapleton's claim repeated
10. implication of litigiousness - PI, Defamation etc
11. Trust 'not taking action' as it might lead to 'potential bankruptcy' of Marianne
12. repeating my 'many informal complaints (CF my informing Mitchell of Howells' many complaints abut me)
13. my complaints 'have been investigated''-
14. also claiming BPS complaint 'resolved satisfactorily' for Howells

Stancliffe wrote to Jerrom in similar tone, after the Dignity, decrying my Tribunal attempts and implying my complaints false [10: Doc G].

Barnes' Witness Statement [22: Doc S5]

Barnes used me as 'unofficial counsellor', relating anecdotes of her mentally ill brother thus delaying me in my work. When I formally complained about Howells, Barnes turned, making untruthful, damaging remarks about how I conducted myself [p2 onwards:]

- was, 'unqualified' and 'should be grateful for the job.'
- did not send in forms; 'often not bother and say she didn't have time' [p
- claimed I, 'deliberately sent expense forms late then laughed about it.'

- claimed I, 'bullied her', later changing this to, 'not bullying but .. manipulative', then later '[Marianne] is trying to get people to feel sorry for her.'
- claimed she emailed a senior Secretary, 'who does [Marianne] think she is, signing herself off like this [i.e. 'author/ counsellor']' . This was altered in a new version, saying the Secretary made the remark.
- claimed I spread, 'racist comment' then wrote to Stancliffe denying she said this [22: Doc S1].

Law's Witness Statement [28: Doc Y]

Law described the situation as, 'a series of trivialities got out of hand' [28: Y, p6, point 6a]. This is close to the overwhelmingly-sad heart of the matter. I expand on this towards the end of this report. Page 6 point 6b is a misnomer: it is not 'my appointment' that was 'not good' but bungling of complaints by HR, denial or obliteration of facts through cover-ups.

> **NB** Little notice was taken of either Millar or Law's statements. Had Howells genuinely felt bullied, harassed, or threatened, Law would have known, being not only Deputy Manager but working in the office immediately next door to Howells. Why would Howells not tell Law about these serious issues? The other claim Howells made, of my I 'refusing training and supervision' - Law was my supervisor and training manager. Howells later had to retract the training and supervision issues, after Amarshi's intervention, but no one checked with Law about the far more serious allegations.

Annette Law tried to be too nice, was blind to bullying, reluctant to perceive staff reactions against A4C triggering fatal stressors. When I tried to talk about problems or rifts, she silenced me, making interpretations such as their being 'newly qualified', my being over sensitive, rather than tackling problems head on. She appeared to completely miss growing discontent that began focussing around me. I observed Howells bullying Law, by making humiliating remarks in front of staff causing Law to cringe, yet Law denied this.

Her reactions to Helen, who came forward July 2019 [16: Doc M1 & Doc M2], reinforces my view of Law's denial. She was not malicious but wanted life perfect. A nice person but a bad manager, which is why Practice Manager Mrs Mott was never disciplined, Eldene left in a stressful state. Vociferous senior Assistant Anita Corfe was told 'repeatedly' about being vociferous [28: Doc Y, p3 point 2K.] yet no action was taken. Law claims no one else made complaints about Corfe, yet colleague Becky Watkins found her hard to deal with too. No one would complain given Law's response to me, which is why staff gossiped to Barnes, knowing she would pass complaints to Howells.

For a psychology department it was dysfunctional, lacking in communication considering we were therapists for mentally unwell patients. Corfe, as senior Psychology Assistant, had to give therapy to paedophiles, so must have been under huge stress. By extrapolation I wonder if she received adequate support or felt she could ask, or instead built up steam she dissipated on subordinates. I believe the latter commonplace in this department.

Other Factors About Dignity Investigation

Whilst witnesses were being interviewed, Spaull wrote to the Board with an article on 'incompetent investigators' [23: Doc T1] before dropping out. Booth [Howells' line manager] took over, very strangely re-appointing Stancliffe to assist, when he presumably was already being considered inadequate to the task.

No close colleagues appear to have been interviewed, nor full time Administrator Dianne Fitchett nor colleagues working directly with me at the evening classes, like Lizzie Cambray or Maggie Davison. Stancliffe hints they had not been prepared to disclose statements but this is unlikely, given his vast efforts to paint me in a negative light, to the point of persuading Howells to make a counter claim of bullying against me. I do not believe Howells felt guilty, so much as panic about being discovered making extensive, serious and false allegations. This would explain her anxiety, requesting the investigation to be concluded very quickly.

I later discovered Mitchell let Booth select witnesses. The staff witnesses were Stapleton and Barnes, though all staff appeared in the content list. It is my belief many refused to take part. Jerrom gave the investigators only six weeks to conclude. It is likely Booth wrote the contents list before Stancliffe's interviews.   From my email to all staff [26: Doc W2], you can see the tiny proportion interviewed.

I was not sent copies of witness statements until over a year after they were made. I never had sight of the still missing final Report, upon which Booth, Jerrom and Stancliffe ruined my career.

Missing Report / Contradicting Reports
Booth claimed to have completed her Dignity Report, claiming I had, 'bullied Dr Howells' [18: Doc O1 - 2] but there was 'no evidence' Howells had bullied me, **ignoring Amarshi's statement to Mitchell** [24: V, p4-5, sub paras 1-7]. This missing report was used as a lever during months I endured ill health, anxiety and depression despite Dr Ochoa's attempted intervention [17: Doc N1 & Doc N2].

The missing 'Dignity' and /or 'Disciplinary' Report[s] were used as the basis to terminate my secretarial contract with CAMHS [described later]. The only version of Booth's finalised Dignity Report, referred to as being read by Jerrom, Stancliffe, Booth, Abigail Moore (Head of Personnel),   remains undisclosed. The only version I was sent is by Booth, entitled, 'Disciplinary Investigation Report',   and comprising a single scurrilous remark by Barnes [27: Doc X3].   This missing report is also referred to in Stancliffe's 'reports' to Andrew Dean [24: U4]and the HPC [20: Q7], following my further attempts to have miscreant staff investigated.

42

Knight wrote to Mitchell on 25th March 2007 [27: Doc X1] asking if I had been sent 'the complete content of the investigation report'. This also implies documents other than the 'witness' statements sent me, a year after they had been compiled. She also wrote, 'unless it has progressed to a Disciplinary hearing, which it had not.' It seems very odd that Booth writes on 18 July 2006, 'I am close to the point of completing the first draft of the disciplinary report but I am doubtful of having a final version ready for the deadline next Tuesday' when Knight wrote 8 months later, on 25th March 2007, of the disciplinary not proceeding. This smacks of fabrication, particularly when this document appears to have been used to block my complaints to British Psychological Society, Health Professionals Council and also to negatively influence the four CE's who have blocked attempts at mediation by my successive MP's.

Even if AWP claimed a disciplinary did not proceed because I walked out, lack of procedural closure was certainly responsible for my being deprived of the temporary post at RuH and more importantly, my full time contract as a Secretary at CAMHS Bath. I find it heinous they refused to conclude a procedure, knowing it would have devastating effects; rendering me unemployed and ruining my future prospects- and all based on cruel lies.

AWP Scupper Alternative Employment
Salisbury NHS Trust

Around the time AWP were bungling the Dignity investigation, I was desperately trying to find an alternative professional post, prepared to move home. I found a similar post at Salisbury NHS Trust, who were also beginning to set up Agenda for Change. Determined to apply early, I spoke to the Manager by telephone, which was unusual for me. He seemed impressed by my experience of A4C and my qualifications. I did not mention the debacle at AWP. He said he would send an application and medical forms and looked forward to seeing me at interview. Not receiving these, I rang a week or so later. He was terse, saying, 'I know Dr Howells,' before rapidly terminating the conversation. When I read Stapleton's statement around 2007, she wrote of travelling to Salisbury with Anita Corfe, who vociferously complained 'all the way [there]' about me. [refer 6: Doc E6]

Part Time Post at Another Swindon Surgery

A similar event happened at another Swindon surgery where I applied for a part time post. The other candidate was Valerie Clark, a sex therapist. Howells was present at the interview. The interviewers terminated my interview quickly, practically closing the door on me. Next day, Howells made an issue about my 'not being offered the post', saying Val, 'was better on the day than you.' She kept looking in my face as if for reaction.

I had a strong feeling I had been, 'set up' and Valerie was selected before interview. Val, whom I had no issues with, unusually, came and hugged me at Uni but looking shell-shocked. This was during the dignity interviews. I cannot interpret these events - not then or now.

Temporary Post at Royal United Hospital Bath [RuH]

Still at University, which was my great solace, I fled to Bath to find work. I can't remember if the temporary post at RuH was before or after CAMHS. I was offered temporary work as a Secretary via Randstat, assisting the Administrator in a small office. This was a backroom job using databases. I can't remember which department. This went well and I hoped to be considered for the permanent post as the Administrator was leaving. A few weeks later, she came into the office and said, 'they want you next door' then left. When I went in, there were two HR officers from AWP, a male and a female. They said I could no longer work there, as I had been 'subject of a 'Disciplinary' at Swindon. Really upset, I argued, saying it was an administrative not professional post but they said I must leave immediately. They were embarrassed. I said I would clear my name and make AWP apologise, then left.

12 December 2006:   Children & Adolescent MH Service [CAMHS]

CAMHS Contract Illegally Terminated [6: Doc E]

This job was before or after the RuH temporary post, both in Bath; I cannot remember which. I needed work. I hoped I would be able to get away from the bad name dumped on me and make a fresh start. I hoped, when the fuss died down, to resume my career - hence ongoing attempts to clear my name which AWP call, 'disparaging the Trust.'

I was offered the CAMHS post as ongoing temporary work by Randstat. Again, it was an administrative not professional post, reception and secretarial work for child psychologists and psychiatrists. Four months later I was offered the full time post and signed a contract, countersigned by HR. Two weeks later, on 12th December 2006, Julie Thomas AWP wrote rescinding the contract [6: Doc E], claiming I had, 'resigned before a Disciplinary'[6: Doc E1] and they received a 'bad reference'. This was suspicious as on 15th December i.e. 3 days later,' Ian Payne of HR emailed Knight and Thomas that both referees were unavailable and he would 'try again next week'[6: Doc Ea]; this correspondence was disclosed by AwP as Part 5, pages 36 -37.

Thomas tried to claim this was an 'initial offer' [6: E1]but we both signed the contract [undisclosed in 2017 but on AWP files for the 2006 Tribunal]. I found the reference which said I, 'did not get on with a member of staff.'

I wrote to Dr Holliday [6: Doc E5], a highly distressed email, copying Dr Farkhani's reference [4: Doc C], reminding him of Mott's hostile attitude to counsellors [W: p3 para 8b] whereupon he provided a new reference [4: Doc C1]. I sent this to HR asking them to reconsider and reinstate the Dignity which was haunting my attempts at professional work. They refused.

I wrote in desperation to CAMHS staff [6: Doc E3]. The last sentence reads, 'I ..do not know, at this moment in time, what I have left to live for'. CAMHS Manager Peter Wilson instructed the professionals not to respond [6: Doc E4]. Were it not for a female psychiatrist disobeying and emailing, 'your character will shine through,' I do not know what might have resulted   [23: Doc T3 p2 - GP Data 20 November 2006, 'on severe mental health register' - disclosed to AWP as batch 1 of 3 GP Data]. I wrote angrily to HR [29 : Doc Z1 p1]. Knight instructed Mitchell, 'put this with the MR papers' [29: Doc Z1, p2].

Dr O'Connor

Still without closure, I asked for a meeting which was set up on 5th November 2007 at the Chippenham office of the Trust. Not long after I entered the room, anxious because of pointing and whispering by Receptionists, O'Connor said to me, 'Don't you feel guilty?' Overwhelmed with emotion, I fled. Later, Knight wrote to Howells and Mitchell, 'she can't seem to let this go' [6: Doc E8] saying she would write to Amarshi, asking if Howells could take legal action against me. The day after, Jerrom too up the same theme [18: Doc O5], ignoring my continual distress, absences with anxiety depression, Amarshi 's statement and Jacqueline Millar's evidence.

I am still shocked that these highly qualified psychologists appeared to have no idea of why closure might be vital for me. It seemed they wanted me to 'disappear' [18: Doc O6].

Refusal of Reference Leading to Blacklisting

On 12th I was sent an email by Director of HR, Julie Thomas saying they would only provide a factual reference which would [not verbatim] 'also include the fact a disciplinary remained unconcluded at the time of your resignation' [6: Doc E1]. They put me in a 'Catch 22':

- I would only receive a loaded reference, impossible for me to obtain professional work;
- this reference referred to a disciplinary which never took place, based on Booth's missing Dignity Report;
- no potential employer would believe me, because senior HR and the Board had been duped and firmly believed Howells' accounts of everything.

HR wrote they would 'circulate every NHS Trust' to inform them I had, 'bullied colleagues.' This was disclosed in 2006 then disappeared. It should be in Palmer's files.

Relationship with Temp Agency Spoiled

AWP contacted Randstat and thereafter the agency did not offer work. Like all temp agencies, they put clients before temporary workers. Randstat was one of few I would term decent, offering higher hourly rate and better contracts with holiday pay. They did not harass you to work during sick leave.

I was now practically unemployable in every area covered by AWP;   most of the South West. It was 2 weeks before Christmas and contracts scarce with so many low paid temporaries seeking work.

Mental Ill Health - Misperceived, Repetitive Emails

By December 2007 my emotions were out of control; signs of autistic breakdown manifested in:

1. emotional swings, with anger, frustration and anxiety freely expressed;
2. longer, detailed emails - cf Amarshi Attendance Note [9: Doc B, p1 para 6, 3- 5]
3. yet unable to make myself understood [6: Doc E4, lower half of page];
4. extreme frustration when not listened to - a very prominent feature of autism
5. repetition, mixing up dates
6. desperate to be heard so sending far more emails, to everyone I thought might respond
7. powerless, saying I would take Court action (to prevent more false allegations), but unable to do so
8. using writing as solace as I always do but with errors, repetition and at a lower level of analysis

During this time I sent an 'offensive email' to HR [30: Doc Trib 2], the only time in my life I have written in such terms. I was in utter despair, wanting to shock them out of silence. I could not understand why an organisation paid £millions to listen to patients could not perceive I had been driven to the same need. I believe this email was bandied such that CE Iaian Tulley wrote to my MP around July 2014, 'you should seen what she wrote,' [undisclosed but in AWP files] as if this were my usual persona.   This was followed by senior staff exchanging disparaging remarks about me, instead of standing back and considering why:

Negative/ Defamatory statements - Dr Anne Booth

[28: Doc Y2] [underlining   is mine - Marianne]

p6, point 19a: 'MR sent an email dated December 23rd whose tone was threatening towards LH' Cf [26: Doc W8] emails between Marianne & Knight, 23 to 28 Dec 2005
p7, point 23a: "AB has <u>no concrete evidence</u> justifying any concerns about MR's practice.   In one or two communications MR has said that the GPs are more than happy with work she has undertaken.   We believe this is not entirely true but the GPs have not been prepared to express themselves in writing.   AB does not know the nature of their concerns.' cf testimonials [26: Doc W5] & [4: Doc C & Doc C1].
p7, point 23b: 'Having read the case report discussed above, AB has concerns about MR's practice.   There is a blurring of MR's needs with the clients needs; MR appears to lack boundaries.   This is the reasonable impression <u>from reading one report only though</u>.   There have been no complaints about her practice.   But extrapolating from her relationships with colleagues gives further cause for concern.' cf [26: Doc W5] Annette Law supervisor reference
p9, point 25i: 'This whole process <u>arguably</u> meets this definition though LH doesn't perceive it this way.   The issue that means that it might not is the issue of <u>maliciousness.   This implies intentionality</u>' Cf Amarshi to Mitchell [25: Doc V, p4-5, points 1-7: also Millar's statement [31: Doc N3]
p10, point 27: '<u>Some</u> of MR colleagues have complained about MR's treatment of them.   This led to AM's investigations etc described above.   <u>Some</u> admin staff have also complained about MR's treatment' [Mitchell offers no concrete evidence; none of these staff interviewed]
p10, point 28a: 'We have a member of staff – MR - who has difficulties in relationships with colleagues and who tends to manage those difficulties by locating them in the behaviour of others.   This is hinted at in her employment reference provided by Wiltshire County Council' Cf [26: Doc W1]: Wiltshire county Council Reference
p9, point 25k: 'Marianne has poured out her distress to others.' Untrue - based on Howells' claims in witness statement i.e. 'spending hours in working time , Cf [26: Doc W4] Zoe Salmon confirms Marianne's usual personality is to reveal personal information
p6, point 21a - b - Booth's response to question '*What Should Have*

Happened Differently?' 21a. 'Retrospectively, in August 2005 there should have been a much more robust and formal response from the Trust (AB, AM, or BJ) to MR's refusal to accept performance management.   This might have resulted in a disciplinary process.   The actual outcome was an ambiguous message for MR about conduct.   There has been a sense of paralysis, as if Personnel and Senior Managers haven't known what to do..   21b. .. nothing else that should have been done differently.   The service has done its utmost to support MR.'

Cf [9: Doc B, p6 para 5] Jerrom admits liability for disability discrimination

Cf [25: Doc V: p4 - 5 points 1-7] Amarshi to Mitchell re trumped up Performance Mgmt

---

p6-7, point 22a - b: 'We considered role of Occupational Health but MR never went off sick for long enough...they were naïve about MR's state of mental health. She needed a specialist assessment.. Perhaps we should have pursued this... Occupational Health ..advice was that she had low self-esteem and her confidence needed boosting.   AB feels there is a personality difficulty'.

Cf [9: Doc B, p6 para 5] Jerrom admits liability for disability discrimination

---

p10 28b: 'MR does not perceive the legitimacy of managerial authority'

Cf [25: doc V p4, paras 1 - 7] Amarshi to Mitchell; also p4 para 2 'why the Trust did not feel it appropriate to take these matters forward with Dr Howells.'

P10, 28c: 'she makes allegations against others or goes off sick to avoid discussion of problems'

Cf [17: Doc N2] Dr Ochoa letter

p10, 28d: 'LH does not perceive MR's conduct as bullying'

cf [25: Doc V1, p2, para 2] Jerrom to Howells, 'I am aware you have felt bullied and intimidated.. personally threatened by her'

P10, 28d: 'LH has always had in the back of her mind that if she puts a foot wrong she could end up in court.   This has led to paralysis.'

? why so fearful of Tribunal.

Defamatory remarks by Dr William Jerrom:

[8: Doc B], Amarshi Attendance Note:

- p3 para 5; 'aggressive refusal to accept reasonable management requests'
- p3 para 6, 'two incidents of racist comments' [cf [22: Doc S1], Barnes rescinds allegations
- p6, penultimate para, 'the claimant is very vindictive and Dr Howells is an exemplary employee whose
confidence and health has been affected by the Claimant's actions'

[18: Doc O5] asking what legal or police action might be taken against me

Defamatory emails sent by Christopher Stancliffe:

[13: Doc J3], **Stancliffe to Booth** []: 'We could get bogged down in a discussion with her about who thinks she has Aspergers ..This will take several months potentially. I think we need to end this now' (also referenced as [30: Doc Trib 1]).

[10: Doc G point 4] 'nor do I even think a Tribunal is likely to take much interest in her case, given she declined to participate in the previous grievance process against Liz'

[10: Doc G, point 7]: 'spoken to Liz .. not informed her of the threats that Marianne makes in her emails below '
[attachments not disclosed]

[10: doc G9, p1 final para]: **Stancliffe to Health Professionals Council:** 'The Trust has reason to believe that provision of these documents to MR would result in further unjustified, but psychologically and professionally damaging complaints being made about its staff. The Trust requests that further disclosures to MR are anticipated and resisted unless legally obliged'.

[10: Doc G10], **emails to Mitchell and Abigail Moore**:

- 'the MR saga continues'
- 'any thoughts you have on potential harassment of Liz'
- 'I worry there may be a lengthy programme of harassment [by Marianne]'
- 'could you ask Swindon OHS to make available [counselling] for Marianne for a couple of months'
- 'I'm up to my eyes in pants'
- 'I'll do a note to those staff who permitted their statements to be released'
  nb. no other 'witness' statements' have ever been disclosed
- Maybe she [Marianne] has said some new stuff in recent days that troubles him [Jerrom]'

Andrew Mitchell , HR Manager of Victoria Hospital

[31: Doc Y1,p1-2 paras i - iii] 'condescending', 'threatening' or 'making veiled threats'

SENIOR HR STAFF 'bored' by Marianne Complaints
[33: Doc Derogatory]

Stancliffe 'the MR saga continues' [doc derogatory]
Julie Thomas 'and the next one..'

Far from the intelligent professional I had been, struggling to treat vulnerable patients under dire conditions, this was the image promulgated and had now stuck: vicious, chaotic, vengeful, verbally abusive, obdurate   - the 'working class thug' Howells wished them to perceive, in her determination to avoid investigation. I had, in other words, lost my identity.

Jerrom again and again asserted I, 'bullied' Howells, despite evidence to the contrary[8: Doc B] & [9: Doc B p 3-5] & [10: Dob G]. I felt helpless, just as Helen R. felt helpless after one attempt at complaining about her treatment. When Barnes retracted her racism claim [11: doc H], no one listened. They had long closed eyes and ears #.

Evidence of Mental Ill Health
Screenprints from GP Surgery at Westbury

My mental health during these traumatic years is clearly portrayed in screenprints of the GP Index Data from Westbury Surgery computer [30: Doc Trib 3, pgs 4-9] which I copied to the memory stick as GP Index Data batches 1 -3]. These are the only GP records in good order; many paper records were missing and every year was   jumbled when I went to retrieve them for Tribunal, as if dropped or someone carelessly riffling through the stack. The GP index charts the course of my mental ill health as I enter Howells' employ, through my employ at B&Q after CAMHS was rescinded, deteriorating with each successive attempt at Tribunal.

From Professional to Shop Assistant

After AWP refused a full reference, spoiled relationswith Randstat, terminated my temp contract then my CAMHS contract, I was forced to seek what work I could. I was offered a night contract at B&Q, as a shop assistant. B&Q is not a good employer. There is a lot of manager bullying as they are pressured from the top of to make profit each week in their department or risk dismissal on some excuse or another. Thus, they pressurise staff to work during sick leave when you are subjected to an intense telephone conversation from 'staff health' [sic] asking you to describe symptoms, explaining why you cannot work and when you intend to return. Union membership is actively discouraged whilst the environment is poor. At bank holidays and weekends, there is presure to work overtime. For someone with autism it is horrendous. There is discrimination against disability and also racism. Wages are low, contracts short, so they can easily terminate a contract and put employees on worse contracts, such as reducing the historic overtime payments for Sundays and Bank Holidays.

However, giving the lie to claims by Howells that I thought certain work, 'beneath' me, I worked hard and received manager testimonials for my excellent customer service [26: Doc W9 & W10]. I also attachd a copy of an old testimonial from the Salvation Army (where I helped with a house clearance for a hoarder whilst working for Buckinghamshire NHs Trust mental Health Team) [26: Doc W11] (my name then being Miriam).

Losing Cottage then Houseboat. Forced into Social Housing

Through to 2009 I was fighting for survival, mentally and financially. Worried about finances, though NOT in debt, I panicked and sold my cottage at a huge loss, it being recession. In 2006, I purchased a houseboat. This was not a 'pipe dream' as I had lived on a boat many years whilst married. Due to the turmoil I was not in a good mental state and purchased inadvertantly from a confidence trickster. I lived aboard some time before the boat started to sink when I took it down river for repairs. AWP knew what was happening because disclosures revealed copies of 2 articles in the Bristol Post [30: Doc Trib4 & Doc Trib4b],which someone had searched and downloaded, probably searching under my name. As these were my last savings, I applied to civil court trying to retrieve some of the £24,000 I paid for the vessel, only to be defeated after three years [30: Doc Trib4 & Doc Trib4b], during which I could not also deal with AWP. To my dismay, the confidence trickster won costs of £19,000 paying his Barrister out of my £24,000 as well as a boat surveyor I knew (*he did not realize the case was about my boat*). The boatmen later told me the conman had bought the vessel for £2900 so he knew it was not worth what he sold it for. I had no legal help and lost the boat. I had to move into social housing be homeless. This is the first time I had lived in social housing.

Stancliffe Derogatory Remarks & Trolling on Internet

Disclosures for 2017 Tribunal revealed a spiteful comment from Stancliffe to HR on the lines of,'she has got herself into difficulties over another court case', again portraying me in a negative light.

There were further derogatory emails, missing in to 2009 disclosures, where Stancliffe wrote about my claims, something like [not verbatim] 'it [my claim] stops a while then starts up again.' See also [10: G10] 'the MR saga continues.'

Stancliffe appears to have relished his role as an 'investigator'. He was trolling me on the Internet. [24: doc : U2] is a fragment of a document, disclosed by AWP as, '2017 02 01 CS notes.' On page 3 there is a heading, **'Not for inclusion in the final draft**.' This page comprises searches for my name, showing my Linked In and Goodreads author pages, with images of my free training course for aspiring writers. I believed he hoped to 'prove' I was recovered, because I was writing this course ie an attempt to deny my mental ill health at Tribunal.

Though Corte and Begum, i.e. regarding 'racist comments' had left the Trust, in June 2006 Stancliffe was seeking their home addresses [24: Doc U6], despite there being no 'witness' statements from either during their employ.

The last is someone, delving into my attendance at BASS, Bath Adult Autisim Services. There is an email I cannot find but Palmer should have, where someone entered BASS records to discover my attendance, then made a spurious conclusion, challenging my autism diagnosis on the basis I was not attending BASS. I complined to BASS about this and received a response, which will be on BASS files.   Later, another spurious claim was made, that I appeared to be, 'strongly resistent' the idea of joint medical experts to re-examine me for autism.

I am unsure how much of this was within his professional province, but I have been very upset by the attempts to delve in my private life, being a very private person. Together with the undignified and horrific claims about harassment, violence   and so on, I feel doubly abused, as if I was being bullied again.

TRIBUNAL ACTION

Summary of Rahim Amarshi Challenges for 2007 Tribunal

Jerrom Denies Autism Diagnosis During Tribunal Preparations

Bevan Brittan of Bristol, attempted to suppress my medical notes from the bundle until I demanded they be put in. I describe this later. Amarshi questioned Jerrom on the latter's reluctance to admit he knew of my autism and subjecting me to gruelling HR procedures against the DDA [9: Doc B, p6, para 5 last sentence].

Amarshi Letter to Mitchell [25: Doc V]

- Amarshi presents evidence the performance management was based on falsifications. He states there is evidence of Howells' bullying staff. He queries why Howells not investigated [25: Vp4,paras 1-7]

Mitchell to Amarshi [20: Doc Q1 to Doc Q7]

- Mitchell claim investigators find 'no evidence' of bullying by Dr Howells [20: Doc Q2, para 2] but vice versa.
- Mitchell wrote Howells never claimed I bullied her # [20: Doc Q2 p2, under 'ET claim form point 5' no 1]
- Mitchell again misrepresents Union meeting [20: Doc Q2, p1 para 3 'in July 2005']

Stancliffe to IT [13: Doc J1 & Doc J2]

- Stancliffe writes to Booth, that only Howells has indicated a threat of violence against staff [Doc J1]
- Stancliffe informs IT Howells & Booth claimed I 'threatened' staff [Doc J2, p1 no 8]

Booth to Jerrom [20: Doc Q6]

- Booth writes to Jerrom 'this email states explicitly that the meeting was convened to express performance issues' - clearly misleading him

Jerrom's description of me in the Attendance Document include, 'very vindictive' whilst describing Howells as, 'an exemplary employee'[8: Doc B, p6, final para]. He also passes Barnes' hearsay about racism, viz:

- Barnes claimed I made 'racist remarks' [22: Doc S5, p2 no 3d]
- trying to rescind this [22: Doc S1].
- Jerrom told Amarshi I made, 'two racist remarks' [8: Doc B p3, para 6] # yet never rescinded this after receiving Barnes' corrections.

Howells to Mitchell [20: Doc Q5]

- Howells forwards my email to Mitchell, reframing this meeting - insisting she had already contacted Unison and was waiting a response [she gave no evidence of this].

Versions of AWP Procedures Following 'Dignity' Interviews

I provided on the memory stick all documentation disclosed by AWP about the dignity investigation. This comprises the interviews but no report. I have never seen, and these have never been disclosed, the documents referred to in correspondence variously as the 'Dignity Report' or 'Disciplinary Report.' The only version of the latter is an incomplete document at [27: Doc X3] containing one vile allegation by Barnes.

There are ambiguous referrals to a 'disciplinary' as follows:

Dr Jerrom claimed I, 'refused to take part in the Dignity' ignoring sick notes lodged with HR [10: Doc G1 to Doc G6], proving I suffered several bouts of depression and anxiety during this employ. Any GP or Psychiatrist will confirm depression takes months or years to recover and for recovery the stressors need to be removed, hence they sign off patients. Jerrom further claimed I 'bullied' Howells and displayed 'aggressive refusal [8: Doc B, p3 para 5] to accept the 'roles and responsibilities of other staff' (referring to my refusal to accept Howells' falsified complaints and ensuing performance management) and that I was suspended [18: Doc O3].

In contrast, a letter from Knight to Mitchell March 2007 claimed the Dignity, 'never proceeded to a disciplinary' [18: O4]. A letter from Booth dated 13th June 2006, annotated 'THIS LETTER WAS NEVER SENT (AJM)' claims a suspension meeting was held in my absence [27: Doc X4]. An email from Stancliffe 9 August 2006 [27: Doc X5], requires me to 'participate in this process' i.e. Dignity at Work, 'as the subject of it' i.e. their assumption I had bullied Howells; further that the, 'process will continue and if appropriate a disciplinary will be held'.

Above documents in date order:			
27 Oct 2005 to 11 Aug 2006	Doc G5	Screenprint from Westbury Surgery	Screenprint from GP records show mental ill health continuous during AWP investigations
Undated fragment - as disclosed	Doc G2	Stancliffe to Spaull assume Marianne refusing participation in dignity investigations	Partial email with proposed letter to Marianne: • ' wouldn't want to put any more pressure on her to participate now than is contained here' • ' **Might turn up a notch later'** • 'not prevented MR discussing her responses with a solicitor'
20 Feb 2006	Doc G1	Stancliffe to Marianne	Jerrom notification of investigation contains Howells' counter claim of bullying
6 Mar 2006	Doc G4	Dr Connell	Marianne sick note 'stress at work, also anxiety and depression'
20 March 2006	Doc G3	Dr Connell	Marianne sick note for 3 weeks 'anxiety and depression'
? 6 June 2006 # ? 12 Aug 2006 #	Doc O3	Jerrom to Marianne	*disclosed doc has 2 dates [i.e. tracked changes]* Jerrom and Abigail Moore reviewed the final report'
13 June 2006	Doc X4	Booth to Marianne	• Annotated 'this was never sent' • x refers Jerrom letter, 'disciplinary to be carried out' • 'you are suspended from work.. while investigation is carried out' • 'must not contact Dr Howells without ..prior agreement of myself or Alice'

9 Aug 2006	Doc G6 Doc G7	Stancliffe to A. Moore A. Moore to Stancliffe	'I suspect I am being toyed with' ' I think you are right!!!!!'
9 August 2006	Doc X5	Stancliffe to Marianne 'blaming' email	'you are being invited to take part in this process as the subject of it'
undated	Doc X3	Booth	uncompleted 'Disciplinary Report'
Sunday 25 March 2007	Doc O4	Knight to Mitchell email	• asking if Marianne 'has complete access to the report prepared by Chris Stancliffe and Debbie Spaull' • 'ask [Amarshi] whether Tribunal gave MR permission to contact staff to seek statements' • 'report would not normally have been disclosed unless it had proceeded to a Disciplinary, which it had not' • requests all further communication via solicitors
29 March 2007	Doc B, p3 par 5	Amarshi Report	Amarshi telephone conversation with Jerrom

Tribunal Procedures

I did not want to undergo Tribunal, and would not have done so had AWP procedures been fair, had they complied with my requests with mediation, and allowed me to refute Howells allegations at an early stage, for example, Had Mitchell or Jerrom listened, none of what followed would have happened. Likewise, had Jerrom listened and acted appropriately, when informed of my initial diagnosis, instead of going into denial. I knew it would be stressful and time consuming with the outcome uncertain, especially as AWP had a legal team, three different ones (but the same Barrister) over the years this went on, whilst I had piecemeal input from solicitors who, naturally, spent minimal time and effort helping a non paying client. All this ended in Barrister Anya Palmer (representing AWP from 2006 to 2017) having EVERY APPLICATION thrown out before I could state my case and present evidence. This means, **I have never had closure**, having to bear the weight of the most vile allegations, defamatory, distressing and humiliating descriptions of me, without the opportunity to defend myself. I was ill, I did NOT avoid the Dignity, which was grossly handled.

There were only so many proceedings because of Anya Palmer abusing law to block me, instead of letting me state my case unhindered. Doubtless she was instructed by Stancliffe to keep my case out of Court at all costs and it is clear why he would have done this. I started proceedings in 2006 but, unable to cope with B&Q, social housing, my emotions, losing the boat after losing my beloved cottage also coming to terms with autism, I asked AWP to settle. I thought I would be able continue my career when I recovered, not realizing this would become impossible due to the harsh conditions AWP laid down, ruining my career but blaming me for my determination to have justice.

Draconian Cot - 3 June 2007

I thought AWP would settle fairly. I did not know what fair settlement meant but I wanted apology, judicial settlement (i.e. compensation to put me where I was before this employ). I wanted to buy another home, retrieve my career and living in dignity. I was only half aware, desperately trying to appear sane, using University and my writing to keep my dignity intact - even this failed.

I signed Cot3 [30: Trib 5] with the aid of a 'free half hour' solicitor; trainee human rights solicitor Nighat Sahi of Christian Khan, London [I was in Batheaston]. Although AWP claim I was in sound mind, no one in their right mind would accept such a paltry settlement and draconian agreement, with vile accusations unchallenged:

- a long list of exclusions, including claims under the disability and employment acts
- a silencing clause - therefore, preventing my relief by, 'telling my story'
- no admittance of liability, no apology
- the investigation leaving a burden of blame on me
- subjected to the most vile, untruthful accusations, including of criminality
- there was no outlet for restoring my good name or retrieving my career
- AND the instigator, Howells, was never investigated

I knew settlement should include disability and hurt, but though they informed my MP Mr Rees-Mogg they included these, this was untrue. I signed Cot3 without reading or understanding it fully. It was neither the fault of ACAS, who had minimal involvement, nor Ms Sahi, who were doing what I asked: to get settlement urgently to relieve my huge emotional distress. Ms Sahi perhaps should have pointed pitfalls, such as not having full disclosure, but AWP had claimed they made full disclosure [doc 30: Trib 17, undated fragment, disclosed by AWP - AWP claim full disclosure has been made]. Ms Sahi did what I asked in a limited time and did not charge. I regret that later I got angry with her. She was a trainee, doing her best. I know Palmer successfully used the defence of non full disclosure in later Tribunals - so how can the law be one thing for one case and then be turned completely around?

Lack of unbiased investigation by the Dignity investigators, reports by Stancliffe to Deputy CE, Andrew Dean [24: Doc U4; (also Dean's letter to Marianne [24: Doc U4a]) - passed verbatim through four successive CE's [Iaian Tulley, Hayley Richards [12: Doc I], Simon Truelove, Dominic Hardisty), resulting in absolute refusal by AWP to investigate, considering Cot3 'closure'

[34: Doc ZZ4].   Maybe for them, but not for me; to this day I suffer from the backlash.

Personal Injury Thwarted

Ms Sahi apparently left provision within Cot for a Personal Injury, which is possibly why she allowed Palmer to include so many exclusion clauses. Yet, such a complex action is impossible for a litigant in person.   I did attempt this but it was a despairingly futile gesture, trounced at the first application by AWP's legal team because I did not get documents registered in time. I strongly remember being distraught and in tears outside Court, where an Usher was comforting me, whilst the young Barrister high fived himself in the car park. This was   one of several of my pathetic 'actions,' paraded by AWP to 'prove' I was maliciously litigious [20: Doc Q7, p3 para 4], instead of perceiving my bumbling attempts to seek justice, my inability to understand rules and procedures pitched against a strong autistic need for understanding and closure. Stancliffe, instead of unbiased professional ism, spread vile hearsay so widely, inside and outside AwP, I could never stem the tide to regain my good name in the mental health field. He was not only unprofessional, but embroiled on a personal level.

10th Aug 2008: Howells Admits Stress in 'The Psychologist'

I discovered this article by Howells online around 2017; published in the professional journal, 'The Psychologist', dated August 2008, volume 23, p624 - 635 [5: Doc D1]. Here for the first time Howells admitted the stress of implementing stepped care and strong opposition to it:

"*We were the first stepped-care service for mental health in the country and back in the nineties it was often a fight to get acceptance*"

Despite awareness of Howells' behaviour, Jerrom put her forward for CBE then later OBE. This was around the time Helen was being bullied [16: Doc M1 & Doc M2].

Attempts at Re-Opening 2006 Tribunal

Shortly after signing Cot3, I emailed HR asking if Howells, Stapleton and Jerrom would apologise for damage to my reputation, loss of career and insults by Howells about my deceased father [30: Doc Trib 8, p1], whom she had claimed within her witness statement had abused me, leading to my spending, 'hours in core time' talking to cOlleagues about it. This again was a wicked lie. I offered to drop any further action if they did so, being concerned with closure more than anything else. Knight and Jerrom had been exchanging emails [30: Doc Trib 8, p2], not about Howells' bullying triggering everything that followed but:

- what action they or Howells could take against me;
- if my emails amounted to criminal harassment;
- wondering why I could not 'let this go';
- discussing what Tribunal might award against me for breaching Cot3

The Applications are on Court records.

2009 Judge Sara

[30: Doc Trib 6 & Doc Trib 6a] In 2008, Judge Tickle gave permission for me to attempt to overturn the Cot 3 [30: Doc Trib 6]. This appeal was to be in 2009 at the Court of Judge Sara in Bristol. AWP tried to block this [30: doc Trib 6b], attempting to nullify my request to present medical evidence of disability [30: Doc Trib 6b]. It did go   ahead without me, as explained below, and Barrister Anya Palmer was successful in claiming to Judge Sara, that I would 'not be able to present evidence of depression and autism,' though I was in Dr van Driel's office 27 May 2009 [30: Doc Trib 7], the day before the hearing, being treated for depression also first stage of diagnosis for high functioning autism (formerly 'Asperger Syndrome'). The Court Clerk rang me so it is recorded in Judge Sara's Judgement on page 2. In view of Judge Sara knowing the above, I was astonished Palmer convinced him to give judgement, though he made this a 'Reserved Order'.

2016 - 2018 Appeals Blocked by AWP Barrister

At 2016, I sent Tribunal a list of all the mediations I had attempted, from 2005 to 2016, including AWP HR and external mediating agencies [30: Doc Trib 11]. What I wanted was to re-instate the 2006 Tribunal i.e. have the Cot3 nullified and a judicial settlement which would be fair, including reparation for hurt and disability, as well as apology for defamation. I had requested and agreed Cot3 under what the Court terms, 'duress' - from my view, the appalling circumstances AwP put me through by bungling; financial pressure; losing a stable career and the promise of a future in research; losing my home; being isolated in the community; the blackening of my character and family name. I am still furious that Howells had made my father out as an abuser to hive off blame and punish me.

This was a load no one could be expected to endure, let alone when preparing for Tribunal and in the face of denial of disability by AwP:- a powerful mental health trust with professionals like Jerrom, Booth and Stancliffe putting loyalty before truth . I would have to face this mountain in order to get before a Judge. I simply found it easier, as do so many victims, to go along with them, hoping they would play fair. I hoped by so doing to maintain my career, proven by the large number of emails I sent AWP shortly after signing Cot3. AWP have copies on file.

I asked Judge if it would not be possible to go back to 2006. I was informed it was not and I must return through applications one by one. Had I had access to continuous legal help this would have been settled in 2006 rather than collapsing under the weight of Palmer's gamesmanship. Repeated and (what I experienced as complex) administrative application, had to be completed in short time frames, for example even the remission of fees and getting together receipts - such rigmaroles adding to the pile of stress. Court procedures might appear straightforward to those familiar with them but not to outsiders, particularly if disabled by autism. I accounted for the huge time gap between applications in a document which Judge never saw [30: Trib 10] viz:

- distressed and muddled by unclear thinking due to mental ill health
- getting over detailed, re-checking, with hours to prepare each document
- consistent refusal by AWP to cooperate
- AWP legal team gamesmanship
- undisclosed documents - constantly having to request these, hampered by my reluctance to use a telephone
- physical exhaustion
- getting an autism diagnosis and the aftershock, trying to come to terms and learn what this meant
- losing two homes in a row, moving to social housing
- financial shortage leading to working at B&Q [less than half professional salary and a stressful environment
- 4 years fighting houseboat confidence trickster before losing with massive costs
- uncertainty about where I would live, the new community and the problem of making new friendships
- losing friends because they were embarrassed, could not cope with my pain, or feared visiting social housing
- culture shock of social housing; being bullied [Keynsham & Stanton Drew police aware], thus moving 3 times

Around 2016, Liam Stallard, the Trust Para Legal, left AWP without notice. I have a strong suspicion this is why I received documents not previously disclosed, i.e. staff dealing with my disclosure request not knowing what, 'should be' held back; the Attendance Note being one such. Stancliffe had offered to help Liam sort documents for this Tribunal [30: Doc Trib 18]. Stancliffe himself provided a statement for 2016 Tribunal, referenced 'M-3582179-3' [30: Doc Trib 19] downplaying his role with wild assumptions e.g. my working at B&Q 7 years as 'evidence' my health was unaffected affected long term by events at AWP .

Having no legal knowledge, I do not know how Palmer succeeded in blocking every application. The following are Tribunal applications, with decisions where I have copies:

65

2016	• **19 Mar 2016** complied with ACAS mediation - AWP refused to participate [30: Doc Trib 9] • 02 May 2016 Marianne's statement to Tribunal [30: Doc Trib 10] • **02 May 2016** ET1 and ET3 from appeal to Judge Livesey at Bristol [30: Doc Trib 10a] • **20 July 2016** - Judge Mulvaney order at preliminary hearing [30: Doc Trib 10e]
2017	• sent Tribunal mediation timeline 2005 to 2016, all thwarted [30: Doc Trib 11] • **08 Feb 2017** Judge Livesey refused my appeal of his judgement [30: Doc Trib 10b] • **02 Mar 2017** Judge Livesey reconsidered, then dismissed me again [30: Doc Trib 10c] • **Oct 2017**; Judge Harper reiterates lost appeals; instructs me not to contact Tribunal [30: Doc Trib 12]
2018	**16 Aug 2018** Judge Fears, acting upon Judge Livesey, dismissed my appeal again [30: Doc Trib 10d] Telephone appeal to Mr Justice Swift - • Promised 1 month from QC under ELAAS- received 1 hour by Barrister before hearing [30: Doc Trib 13] • Judgement of Mr Justice Swift [30: Doc Trib 14]

2006 - 2009: Summary of Periods of Anxiety/ Depression [30: Trib 15]

[30: Trib 15] is a summary, extracted directly from my GP Index Data records, covering July 2006 to March 2009. It includes GP comments on the nature of my illnesses; anxiety or depression connected with bullying at work.

AWP Illegally Access GP Medical Records & Trolling

During these applications, AWP were illegally access GP and medical records, attendance at the Bath Adult Autism Services [BASS] with Stancliffe trolling me over the Internet.   Someone illegally accessed notes and discharge notes from Green Lane Hospital, Devizes   where I was sent after developing a toxic psychosis after a breast operation - referred to in GP notes as '?pharmacist dispensing incorrect medication '. I had never seen my Green Lane records so this was gross intrusion. This sequence is shown below:

1.   Dr Holliday and Westbury medical records [24: Doc U1]

2. Howells claimed Dr Holliday offered to contact my GP, 'as he knew him ' [26: Doc W, p5 point 16a]:
3. Mitchell apologies for Howells attempt to speak with my GP [Doc U1, p2 par 5] refer 6b below
4. Mitchell 'explains' Howells referring me to Occupational Health three times [Doc U1, p2 par 4]
5. Brenda Moore, claims to be psychiatrist working as a psychologist at AWP
6. Howells attempting to access my records :
    a. [24: Doc U1, p2 par 5];
    b. [26: Doc W, p5 point 16a]; Howells counters no 3 by claiming Dr Holliday made this approach
    c. [23: Doc T3, 2nd entry] unknown staff member enters my GP data index #
7. 13 Oct 2006, GP data extract no 1 of 3, p2, records accessed by unknown staff #
8. Stancliffe includes screenshots of my online writing course,   presenting this as 'evidence' I have recovered from depression [24: Doc U2]- fragment disclosed by AWP as 'CS notes for statement,' dated 1st Feb 2017
9. illegally accessed medical notes from Green Lane Hospital [24: Doc U3 & Doc U3a]
10. Stancliffe re BASS - emails will be on BASS files

The following screenshot [GP Index Data 2 of 3 p14], 'Reminders, is a GP request for staff not to disclose my medical history over the telephone to any other health care staff.

Notes: Breast neoplasm screen (& [mammography]) - Breast neoplasm screen

Cancellation Reason: Patient deducted.

24 Jul 2015	Diabetes 2 month	Superseded on 07 Oct 2015
	Notes: 2mths review good beginning, weight loss, no hypos	
07 Oct 2015	Diabetes 2 month	Seen on 14 Jun 2016
	Notes: trial off gliclazide, declined statins at present, booked for fasting bloods in December	
23 Dec 2015	Diabetes 6 Months	Pending, Due 23 Jun 2016
	Notes: will probably want to Convaersation MAp Education session next year	

Reminders

06 Mar 2015	Large Notes Saltford 6/3/15	Normal Priority
19 Mar 2013	please do not give any information over the phone to any other health care workers (including mental health team) without Mariannes express permission	Normal Priority
16 Jan 2013	This patient is newly registered here, make sure that patient data already on the system has been checked for conformity to policy.	Normal Priority
	double appts for next appt please (MB 11/7/09)	Cancelled on 19 Mar 2013
	Also do not give any info over the phone to other health care workers (including members of comm Mental heath)	

Vaccinations

| 1978 | BCG 1 | BCG |

2017 - 2018 FOI Disclose Previously Withheld Documents

It was not until 2017 - 2019 I discovered the extent of Howells' fabrications. New disclosures sent as new FOI officers came into post. This gave the lie to a letter by Stancliffe to Deputy C.E. Andrew Dean [24: Doc U4] containing untruthful or misleading information:

1. claiming full disclosure had been made [24: Doc U4]
2. The 'Metherall Report' refers to an investigation ordered via BANES Health Commissioners which never took place - see 'BANES Commissioner Investigation - Alan Metherall'.
3. there was no mention of the missing final Dignity or Disciplinary reports
4. Tribunal hearings were misrepresented as my being litigious
5. no mention of Amarshi's findings;
   a. Howells false claims [25: Doc V, p4 paras 1 - 7] and trumped-up performance management
   b. why Howells was not investigated [25: Doc V: p4, pnt 2]
6. no mention of Millar's corroboratory statement [17: Doc N3]
7. a loaded claim about settlement 'being less than court costs' [24: Doc U4, p3, par 4]

New disclosures revealed the shocking claim by Howells, repeated by investigators, that I, 'threatened staff with physical violence [13: Doc J1 & Doc J2] also [14: Doc K]. The Head of Psychology did not comment on anomalies between Howells' increasingly bizarre claims [15: Doc L1] and a glowing Testimonial she provided weeks earlier, before she realized I would not cover up her bad behaviour in exchange for career enhancement.

Further Victims Come Forward After Appeals Tribunal
July 2019 Testimony of Victim Helen of Bullying in 2008

I received testimony in July 2019 from Helen, an ex-employee of the same department, who has epilepsy. She saw my campaign and emailed her experience of Howells in 2008. Helen gave permission to copy her correspondence to anyone concerned [16: M1, M2]. In July 2019 she made a complaint to AWP but after initially promising to call back they ignored her. Shortly after Helen had a seizure, which she had not had for years. For this reason I will not contact her unless positive news. However I left her email address on the documents to prove this testimony genuine.

2017 Callington Road - T. Falsely Accused of Sexual Harassment

T. has not given me a signed statement of his testimony as he still works for AWP. T informed me of false accusations against him at a department of Callington Road Hospital, the hospital being overseen by Dr Jerrom in his capacity of Manager. I have included this information as this will be the last chance I have to give the complete structure of what happened, with the few brave enough to relate their experience of AWP:

I met T. shortly before moving away from the area covered by AWP. I asked if he had any experience of AWP at Victoria Hospital, before and after we were peer students at Uni of Bath. He is career minded, honest and a family man. T. talked of the regime after Howells left, Stapleton now being lead clinician with a peer student of ours, Valerie Clark, promoted by her:

1. weak mismanagement
2. focus on salary and promotion rather than patient care
3. reported Stapleton saying:,
   - 'you are either one of us or not'
   - denigrating his status 'you only drive a white van' wanting him to join them at Victoria Hospital
   - offering 'jump promotion' i.e. jumping several grades

T. informed me that CQC have a department of Callington Road Hospital in 'special measures' with students of long standing not knowing if their training will continue or if their department will be super ceded. T. is in stress because of unfounded accusations of sexual harassment, the complainant failing to make a statement whereas T. was put on garden leave investigated. This incompetent handling of HR procedures mirrors mine.

I have another statement from a former professional at Victoria Hospital, who reports of, 'weak management.' I have her emails on file and prepared to disclose them for verification. There is anecdotal evidence on the Internet, within websites which encourage employees to rate their employers.

70

AWP's Injurious HR Processes
Misrepresented Investigations / Withheld Documents
The Metherall Report [ZZ3, p5, last para] or 'Mr Metherall's Response' [Doc ZZ1] has never been disclosed to me; it does not appear on any of the AWP lists for Tribunal. Metherall did not adhere to Ms Morley's instruction to conduct a new investigation; interviewing me, taking my evidence, providing myself and BANES a copy of his report.

Likewise, Booth's Dignity or Disciplinary Report was never disclosed, though referred to often by Stancliffe. Stancliffe asked IT to withhold documents, claiming fear of my reaction. His sole foundation for this are the falsehoods from Howells and later Booth, which he is responsible for spreading across HR and to the Board.

Both the hearsay and withholding of documents triggered lasting hostility by four CE's who have never met me - relying on Stancliffe to report truthfully and his colleagues to do the same. Fifteen years on, I remain anxious about the nature of these reports, which had such devastating, lasting effects on my life and career.

Attitude
Stancliffe's perspective as HR Business Manager is odd, for example in claiming psychologists are truthful <u>because</u> they are psychologists (33: Doc Derogatory 2]. This attitude circumvents anyone checking the veracity of complaints. This is dangerous in a Mental Health Trust where reports must be impartial and equitable.

AWP's Poor Handling of Complaints
By examining local press reports and online it is easily proven AWP has :
1. been the subject of many negative remarks and actions by CQC
2. received many patient complaints
3. has a high patient suicide level
4. set up a staff anti bullying line in 2017 after my campaign, which should have been in place for years
5. ignore complaints by not responding - e.g. Ms Millar, myself and Ms Ruddock

6. reduced public question time in Board meetings from 30 to 10 minutes with questions in writing beforehand
7. they claim their online database records all complaints i.e. accountability. My complaints do not appear in the database.

FAILURE OF EMPLOYMENT 'HELP' AGENCIES

With my bundle for the 2018 Tribunal, again scuppered by Palmer, I included a list of the mediations I had attempted, internal and external, up to this Tribunal [30: Trib 11]. Since then, Mr Rees-Mogg has written on my behalf 7 times and Mr Heaton-Jones twice [*before the December 2019 elections unseated him*]- all to no avail.

Complaints to CE's:

Iaian Tulley, Hayley Richards, Simon Truelove, Dominic Hardisty

I steadily pursued complaints through successive CE's, meeting the same resistance with CE's relying on Stancliffe's false information including what was termed, 'two professional investigations' - i.e. the bungled Dignity at Work and Metherall's non existent investigation. Hayley Richards response is at [34: Doc ZZ4] and Dominic Hardisty (current CE) at [34: Doc ZZ8].

I will give one example; my letter to Andrew Dean (Deputy to Iaian Tulley) [34: Doc ZZ2]. Stancliffe provided Dean with 'information' [34: Doc ZZ3], referring to 'the Metherall Report' [*see below*], the report which no one, including myself, has seen, has never been disclosed and of which CCG do not have a copy. I have never met this Metherall nor has he ever contacted me.

Stancliffe [34: Doc ZZ3, p5 of 7, final para], "*I understand that, prompted by Ms Richards, an investigation was commissioned by a CCG into relevant concerns. I understand that this did not lead to findings of fault. I understand that this investigation was known at the Metherall Review. I assume that no failing on the part of AWP was identified in this process*".

PALS

It is unclear who is responsible for investigating AWP. AWP website states it is PALS - referred to elsewhere as 'AWP Complaints'. PALS Manager, Jo Collins, sent my entire correspondence to AWP Para Legal, Liam Stallard, without permission whilst failing to respond to my repeated requests for a new investigation. It is unclear from AWP website how 'AWP Complaints' and PALS are linked or if they are one and the same. Such lack of clarity is not helpful to victims in distress.

I contacted PALS on Rees-Mogg's advice but after initial correspondence Manager Jo Collins refused to respond. I find it shocking our correspondence was forwarded as a batch in August 2016, to AWP Para Legal, Liam Stallard # [34: Doc ZZ1 & Doc ZZ1a] but I was not asked or even informed. This request was presumably in connection with a Tribunal. I do not know if this is standard practice but would have objected to maintain confidentiality. This mirrors medical notes being illegally accessed also trolling of my private and business life by Stancliffe. It also mirrors AWP staff asking Whistleblower Guardian, Petra Freeman, to name staff who went to her for advice, which advice is supposedly confidential.

PALS knew I had special funding for psychotherapy; Jacquie Ayres, Complaints & PALS Manager signing 24 Mar 2015 [1: Doc A8a, p8] and 14 June 2016 [1: Doc A8a, p8]. On the agreement for 15 April 2016 the signature page is missing. As the PALS notes were disclosed to Liam Stallard, it is astonishing that at 2017 Tribunal Barrister Anya Palmer did not admit this evidence - i.e. another Tribunal where I did not have the opportunity of proving my mental ill health was because of Manager bullying and bungling by HR.

BANES Commissioner 'Investigation'

In 2016, I corresponded with a BANES Health Commissioner, Andrea Morland (RIP). Morland obtained special funding for me for psychotherapy [1: Doc A8, A8a]; this was to keep my therapy outside the influence of AWP. I was in psychotherapy over two years. Morland agreed to set up an investigation about my treatment at AWP. She tasked this to new AWP employee, Alan Metherall, who was instructed to interview me, read my evidence and re-examine existing evidence, giving her & myself a copy report. Sadly, Mrs Morley died shortly thereafter.

As I had not heard from Metherall, I emailed Val Janssen (Deputy Director of Nursing & Quality) and George O'Neill (Head of Mental Health). Janssen and O'Neill agree to meet so I could outline the history of events, which no one had yet heard. They attended Bath Council offices with a note-taker, where I gave them a power-point presentation [34: Doc ZZ5]. When I talked of my suicide attempt they were agitated, standing and asking if I needed a break. I said I did not but it was clear they wished to leave. They asked what outcome I wanted. I said at minimum written apology and a full NHS pension, settled under NHS Complaints. They promised to investigate. Before leaving, Janssen asked me if I had, 'exhausted all possibilities' for Tribunal and I said I had.

34: Doc ZZ1 is BANES Commissioner Elaine Tubbs' response, headed 'BANES CCG PALS ref 299':
1. say AWP refuse to accept this as a 'new' claim and will neither investigate nor provide information
2. that they have no role as they were not the employer
3. their role was to 'ensure AWP provided [myself] with a response' - [see 1.]
4. that they approached ACAS, who advised BANES had no legal standing to insist AWP replied
a. and that it 'becomes a legal matter for the individual concerned'
5. reiterating this is, 'an historic matter relating to yourself and your employment at AWP'
6. 'BANES CCG remains satisfied with the response provided by Mr Metherall of AwP'

Note point 6 - **'Mr Metherall's response'**, or as Stancliffe terms it, 'The Metherall Report [34: Doc ZZ3, p5, last para] - **nothing from Metherall has been disclosed,** to me, Tribunal, nor AwP disclosures.

Whistleblower Guardian

I presented to the new Whistleblower Guardian, the first incumbent, Petra Freeman, using the presentation given to BANES Commissioners. Although she gave a far more empathic response, this eventually fizzled out under 'lack of funding' to investigate, 'historic cases.' I wrote several times before giving up. In the interest of Justice, I will reveal what Petra told me in confidence - AWP asked her name staff making complaints; in other words, asking her to breach victims' confidentiality in AWP's own interest.

INDEPENDENT REPORT;
'Falsification/Alteration of Documents at AWP' dated 2012
Addendum to above. Whilst writing this report, I searched documents given the Whistleblower Guardian and found this

among files I gave Ms Freeman on a memory stick. I don't know how it became included - possibly Ms Freeman investigating parallels but forgetting to remove it. This report appears to confirm my personal experience. Here disclosed as]document [34: Doc ZZ6]

Union Intervention

Unison representative, Jim D'Avila was helpful. Yet he too had been influenced by Howells when she informed him she was 'worried' that I, 'refused to attend training and supervision'. He admonished me, saying even he had to attend training he did not wish to. It took some time to persuade him he had been duped. This shows not only potential for bias but how easy it is to negate a victim's every potential avenue of complaint.

British Psychological Society

With permission of AWP, I sent a complaint to BPS about Howells claim of re-writing essays, implying plagiarism and risking my Degree being invalidated. I wanted the Degree so much I did not want to lose it on a falsehood. With hindsight I should have complained of her promulgating falsehoods, which AWP was failing to deal with.

I know from disclosures Booth and Jerrom wrote to BPS (undisclosed). BPS concluded my complaint was unfounded, I believe because I did not approach this in the right way. This might seem a small matter but shows how desperate I was to find Justice, but blocked at every avenue by negativity now firmly attached to me with little hope of removing it. In summary, it is very difficult for victims to present a case during trauma, with out extensive help that is not widely available.

Care Quality Council

I made numerous reports to CQC, probably too many with overlong documents as I was still extremely distressed. I reported :

1. falsified reports,
2. professionals being automatically believed,

3. my Manager telling lies and providing false information thus -
4. corrupting internal investigation carried out by her peers, therefore subject to bias.

Though sympathetic, CCQ claimed it was 'not their remit' to investigate individual claims of staff-on-staff bullying OR individual claims of patient-on-staff bullying. The head of CQC recently wrote in the national press, how CQC in future cannot divorce staff on staff bullying from poor care of patients. I asked to be put in touch but no response. I think this a vital measure CQC must acquire, if this role is not taken by your office.

My voluminous, often angry correspondence over time has not been helpful, albeit symptomatic of typical autistic reaction to stress. I have written to CQC to apologise for the volume but explaining I am attempting to show them how easily AWP avoid responsibility and fix blame.

NHS Complaints
I discovered NHS Complaints by accident. No one referred me to this agency which offers 'fair compensation' for victims of the NHS, patients and staff. When I asked Mr Rees-Mogg, he said I would need a solicitor to present my case. I contacted NHS Complaints explaining I had no money for a solicitor. Though they provided a list of schemes like the Bar Pro Bono Unitt, by dint of application, I discovered all the suggested agencies sent you in circles; each so narrow in remit no one fitted your particular situation. This was exhausting as you had to repeat information, fill in more forms, each taking you back through distressing emotions to no effective outcome. I asked for their head of department contact so I could discuss this lacuna (in my self appointed role as anti bullying campaigner) but received no response.

'Tribunals Deal with False Criminal Offence Claims'
(police advice)
I sent copies of emails accusing me of criminal activity to Keynsham police. I informed them the attacks resulted in a nervous breakdown and suicide attempt. I asked if malicious claims added up to disability discrimination, I being autistic and Howells a psychologist and aware of the condition. The police informed me there was no specific law against bullying, this being

covered by existing laws. They said my claims were connected with work, not the result of hate crime attributable to autism and her behaviour fell under the jurisdiction of Employment Tribunal. I took this higher but clearly the officer was annoyed and I never received a response from the senior officer. This added to my frustration and distress.

University of Bath

During 2006 - 8, University of Bath had refused to pass my appeal to alumni for support, because I wrote of my suicide attempt, which panicked the young Alumni admin officer. This has now been righted and I am grateful for them passing my request even at this late stage. This garnered three responses, all critical of AWP, one agreeing to meet me but the others refusing to allow me to pass on their names.

IMPACT STATEMENT
'When all is makeshift /Art cannot bring peace' - 'Too Late' by Iris Murdoch

By the time I walked out of Victoria Hospital on GP advice I had suffered many losses and humiliations:

- my prized mental health career - a life's work, taking decades to amass the knowledge
- loss of my longed-for PhD, now irretrievable and an MSc. which is of no practical use
- the loss of a potential late-life career in mental health research, and the loss of use of the libraries and databases to which I no longer had access, being out of the employ of AWP
- humiliation of being virtually frogmarched out of Royal United Hospital, in front of a colleague
- ditto, deprived of my secretarial contract at CAMHS in Bath where I had started to stabilise
- being made virtually unemployable even as a 'temp'. Losing face with my long term Agency, Randstat
- humiliated by senior staff in many derogatory emails between staff / departments
- been blamed for everyone's grudges, errors of judgement and their rejection of Agenda for Change
- NEVER RECEIVED PROPER CLOSURE, APOLOGY OR REPARATION

The mountain of denial of my autism and depression by senior medical staff of the Trust [30: Trib 16], rendered it impossible for me to oppose them without expensive medical experts and legal input. And not least, the impact on my private and writing life; losing out on contracts, time to market my work, of my inability to write clearly, of a biography of James Sadler I researched for 10 years during this time, only for two other authors to get in before me. All this is beyond price but would have been eased by admission of wrong doing, a sincere apology and fair compensation as set down in law - not AWP's punitive settlement.

Settlement was £12,000, less than a year's salary. My cottage in 2017 was worth around £200,000 and I would have finished paying the mortgage. Stancliffe later wrote disparagingly they made, ' an administrative settlement, less than court costs'. Amarshi verified AWP would not settle the amount set by law: [quote] '..**point of principle of not paying the claimant because we believed that she behaved badly and we were right to do what we did**' [2: B, p6 penultimate para]. This was rough justice after my unnecessary suffering, particularly as they never meant to continue investigations, saddling me as scapegoat without closure.

Metaphor: It is as if I have been in prison since 2006, with no release date.

I am on a lower pension than I should, less of a life than I would have enjoyed given my Masters Degree and the hard work input towards a career. I asked many times for a full NHS pension and the means to purchase a pet as I was socially isolated. All requests were ignored. I had been hounded from AWP, Salisbury NHS Trust, Royal United Hospital, CAMHS [6], had my relationship with Randstat ruined, wrecking my chance of quietly working outside my profession whilst I continued studying and writing. I went on to lose my home, my replacement houseboat home, became depressed then a breakdown. At a low ebb I attempted suicide [7]. The worst were AWP denying my depression and autism; Howells, Jerrom, Booth & Stancliffe making untruthful, highly humiliating remarks, passing hearsay to the CE and Board. In short, I lost my identity.

HOW NHS VICTIMS ARE FAILED

Investigatory Bodies Fail Victims

In my experience, help agencies set up to help victims of employment injustice, at AWP and other NHS Trusts, perpetrate victim suffering. By help agencies I mean senior HR, CE's, Union officials, PALS, CQC, BPC and employer legal experts. They make assumptions, over-trust reports by professionals, show bias in favour of known contacts and want quick solutions (e.g. Jerrom's instructing staff to complete the Dignity investigation in six weeks).

You see, **it is not only toxic staff that prevent justice** but the way investigatory agencies are set up. There are black holes in and between agencies through which victims fall. **Metaphor:** look at the stars and you recognise 'constellations.' Many believe these genuine links, yet they are spurious patterns created by ancient astrologers. Only by getting through the ionosphere do you realize there are light years between stars and star systems; no links, no communication, no similarities. That is my experience of help agencies, including Tribunals.

Differences of Class, Culture or Disability

Victims from the working class are easily misunderstood by middle or upper class professionals. I know this from a friend, long deceased, who voiced negative, incorrect opinions about the motives of young men he sentenced as a Magistrate. I sometimes use vernacular when in deep distress, or frustrated because I do not feel heard. My reactions are passionate but that does not mean I am violent, racist or a thug.

In distress, like many people, I lose my use of language and the ability to think succinctly and speak objectively. Hence, AWP's constant refusals literally sent me insane. Silence or inaction or believing no one is listening does anger victims; relatives of Hillsborough are still angry at no closure 25 years on, yet people wonder why they cannot 'let go'. Proper closure is vital, as I want to express later. Legal professionals play on angry reactions, and it is easy for them to misrepresent claimants, as AWP misrepresented me, simply by pointing to one document in a pile. It is like taking one blemished apple and despoiling the whole barrel by claiming the fruit is rotten. We are all blemished in some way are we not, even Judges?

Autism and Other Little Understood Mental Conditions

Autism is an elephant in the room. Howells' supporters were determined to deny my autism whilst distorting its features 'as if' I am a renegade by nature. Truth is, most agency and Tribunal staff including Judges lack knowledge of the effects of autism; can be easily hoodwinked by persons who have a lot to gain by doing so. There are links on this document [35: Video 1] to information and videos about autism, from the National Autistic society. These highlight errors promulgated by Jerrom, claiming to be expert in autism but misleading Rahim Amarshi. I would have expected different treatment after Jerrom, Booth and Howells knew, but there was more of the same.

There are hidden disabilities, of which autism is one. Only true experts like Tony Attwood, Simon Baron-Cohen, Temple Grandin or Pressure Groups like National Autistic Society can be relied upon for unbiased opinion.

Ignoring Victims' Evidence

I gave Jerrom a fat file of testimonials from employers, patients and clients, proving me as keen, wanting to learn, giving my best. The thread running through is my difficulty communication with colleagues, a clear indication of my later-diagnosed autism. Yet he ignored these, telling HR they were, 'irrelevant.' He also ignored two videos about my time at University, one presenting to peers [35: Video 2], the other after I handed in my Dissertation [35: Video 2b]. Again, these were ignored.

Again, this demonstrates how easy it is for internal investigators to set aside evidence, on the basis it does not correlate with biased opinion about the victim.

Why Victims & Bystanders Fail To Come Forward

Other victims observe suffering by whistleblowers and remain bystanders. Any decent person would be terrified of coming forward if they feared suffering or loss of career, no matter the time gap. I tried to encourage senior counsellors to come forward to testify about AWP under A4C, but no response. And these are professional mental health workers. It was the same with CAMHS staff, where Manager Peter Wilson instructed them not to respond to my appeal, despite the last line clearly indicating I was suicidal.

Perceptions
People perceive things differently, for example Stapleton perceiving University debating as personal criticism of her work. Or Barnes crying, after refusing to call in Health & Safety about my slip in the car park   and I called in Paul Daniels, later receiving thanks for this. Barnes perceived me usurping her authority as departmental Safety Officer. A fair stance depends greatly on a potential Upstander's emotional intelligence or detachment to see past what seems obvious at first view. Side taking is the worst part of victimisation, leading to isolation.

Lengthy Waits for Justice
Victims can wait years, even decades, without getting further forward. This renders us socially isolated, bitter, angry, feeling justice has passed by - cf families of victims of Jimmy Savile, Dr Shipman or the tragedy at Hillsborough. If victims are not extremely resilient, they give up. Who wants to spend a life campaigning? I did not, except for autistic determination (reframed by Jerrom as, 'persistent, disrespectful and rude'), a strong sense of justice and the ability to focus down on a single topic for long periods of time.

Yet, it is vital for victims to be heard. Lack of victim data leaves help agencies bereft of statistics, proper research difficult to quantify, leading to lack of resources and knowledge. For example, the monster of workplace bullying in the NHS only recently raised its head in the press, yet this monster is very, very old (*if you read historic documents or historic novels in the right way*).

Secondary Bullying
Post bullying-bullying (or 'secondary bullying') is perpetration of bullying, either deliberate (sadism) or unwitting (failing to respond, misconstruing). I also experienced secondary bullying in Tribunal processes - harrowing, time-expensive, energy-depleting, confusing, isolating and frustrating. I hope

this does not appear rude, but unless you know how it feels, you cannot act on information.

SUMMARY

I observed bullying in many organisations. I too was naive, afraid, did not have the words or capacity or clout to do anything. As I see it, these issues prevent victims speaking out:

1. internal HR investigatory systems allow rogue staff to manipulate processes;
2. without experience of bullying or knowledge of the dynamics, HR staff assume 'anger' from victims in-built, not   the result of frustration, stress and being bullied: therefore refuse to listen ('stonewalling)
3. HR & CE's ignorant of the dynamics of bullying - e.g. Mitchell calling me, 'arrogant' and 'condescending for sending him Tim Field's, 'Bully Insight'
4. rivalry or disconnection between agencies - one assuming another 'deals with' certain issues
5. 'urban myths' or outdated information - e.g.
    a. nearly every agency, including Tribunal, assume CAB offers free legal advice, legal aid or legal input - funding was removed years ago
    b. that there is extensive free advocacy available - this is severely limited in reality
6. false trust in professionals e.g. Stancliffe's assumption psychologists tell the truth per se.
    Fact: an AWP psychologist sacked for downloading child pornography

HOW TRIBUNALS FAIL VICTIMS

"The Department for Business said in a statement: "Through the Equality Act, employees are protected against harassment in the workplace on the grounds of gender, race, disability, religion or belief, sexual orientation or age, and workers have remedies against this behaviour in the employment tribunals."
https://www.bbc.co.uk/news/business-50436312

'No one stands up for himself and everyone just pays for someone else to do it for him'. Seneca.

'If they can afford to.' Marianne Richards

Legal professionals use methods which further traumatise victims, perhaps not deliberately but learning such methods during training or copying peers:

- employers not forwarding vital documents to their legal team - not queried by latter
- what seems quibbling over disclosure [30: Doc Trib 20 **#**] i.e. I assume dates set by court are end dates, not exact dates on which forms must be presented - muddling for stressed victims to have to keep asking
- employer misrepresenting victims by passing assumptions on to legal experts i.e. biased opinions:
    - legal experts having no duty to repair such assumptions
- gamesmanship over administrative matters e.g. expiry of term for applications, obfuscation of legal terms or procedures, misguidance over bundle content for advantage (e.g. not knowing court applications did not count in bundle, limited number of evidence documents presented
- delay, obfuscating or hiding documents - unknown by whom, but vital reports missing
- suggesting there will be, 'punitive costs, refusal of references, implication of blacklisting
- hectoring or confusing victim: e.g.
    - Solicitor James Gutteridge presenting me with a long 'skeleton argument' as we entered court
    - Paralegal Liam Stallard refusing documents required **#**

- challenging medical experts in court - thus experts reluctant or refusing to act as 'expert witness'
    - (anecdotal evidence of experts made to feel foolish and thus losing professional face
- knowing victims unable to pay for medical reports or experts -playing on that; for example by constantly challenging victim to provide evidence at an impossible level
    - case in point - Jerrom's misnomers about autism, their considering the hire of another medical expert, after I had been put through trauma and diagnosed by a Consultant Psychiatrist
- expecting victims in trauma to prepare complex bundles, write statements such as this, find supporting documents from huge piles of documents and make a coherent case to the high standard required
- being deliberately overloaded with documentation by legal experts
- abusing victims such that they lose confidence:
  e.g. I was called, 'ludicrous' by a solicitor during the boat case, because I said he was, 'game playing' by delaying documents - 'game playing' is a term from Eric Berne's 'Transactional Analysis.' I realize now he did not know this but there was no excuse for the insult

- fear among barristers of pointing out 'ruling errors,' in case their career or future rulings are affected
    - ELAAS Barrister reluctant to reveal ruling error; asking me not to give his name in court
- Courts not allowing victims sufficient recovery time to respond rationally;
- 'gamesmanship' /specialist knowledge used against victims
- unworkable law; e.g. if you do not know x [point of law] you can be penalised for breaching, ignoring or failing to understand it. #

Metaphor- *you might be able to drive but if asked to participate in Formula 1, you would kill yourself in an F1 modified car. That is, a litigant-in-person does not have equal skills to an experienced barrister, whether preparing a case or presenting in court.*

- lack of awareness of the dynamics of bullying :

This is a vital issue and I would like to give a further example of my distressed emails being misconstrued. This is highly embarrassing as I re-read it today, being recovered from mental trauma to a great extent.

Background : [refer to 33: Doc Derogatory 3 & Doc Derogatory 3b]
The above sequence starts with an angry communication I sent to Mrs Longbottom, Chairman of AwP. At the time I was writing an 18th century novel (now published) hence the historic term, 'jade.' I wanted Mrs Longbottom to understand that because 3 people claim something, it does not mean it is true. This referred to the untruths told by Howells then passed to HR by Booth and Jerrom. Like all my communications in extremis, I worded it very badly (losing control of language) but the email was not intended as insulting.

When I wrote the email, I was working at B&Q. I was not used to working in such a public environment; highly stressful for anyone with autism. I had lost my home, then my houseboat, moving to social housing. I was trying to cope with my late-life diagnosis of autism. My debacle with AWP was ongoing as they refused to listen. On 13th December 2011, a month after my email, Dr Wernham wrote to The Bridge, Wells to get support for me (referred to The Bridge, Wells not Bath CMHT, as I rightly feared AWP staff would illegally access my medical records). Bullying had been going on some time at B&Q, not me, but triggering bad memories of Howells behaviour, the bad atmosphere at Victoria Hospital and Eldene Surgery.

Longbottom, instead of perceiving mental unwellness and offering support, forwarded this to AWP Solicitor, Caroline Saunders. Saunders passed it to Stancliffe with a critical remark, requesting he forward it to HPC. She clearly took personal umbrage, instead of acting professionally.

A month previously, Stancliffe sent a long 'report' to HPC repeating old hearsay, thus biasing my complaint against Jerrom and Booth.

I was naturally angry, expending huge energy compiling reports whilst mentally unwell, blocked by the staff who had escalated the problem in the first place, instead of insisting on mediation from the start - the Trust's own policy for disputes.

Lack of Resources for Victims
Administrative Resources
Legal professionals have Secretariats, computer equipment and expertise on tap. Victims are expected to provide documentation, medical evidence and expert witnesses; resources not affordable to someone who has lost a professional income.   Judges assume legal advice is available. They assume ACAS or other charities help victims when they do not, which I explained in the Agencies section.

Urban Myths of 'Free Legal Advice'
- CAB funding for legal advice was cut years ago
- Law centres are rare and cover small catchments by postcode
- Bar Pro Bono offer 3 days maximum - not time for a complex or ongoing case
- 'free half hour' no longer exists. Such firms were mainly seeking clients for winnable cases
- legal advice via car or house insurance is basic, insufficient to prepare for Tribunal
- County Court Judge in Bath [verbatim], ' they [Barristers] refuse cases they consider unwinnable'

ELAAS Insufficient
I was 'offered' a month's work by a QC for my final appeal. What I actually received was an hour just before my telephone hearing with Mr Justice Swift. The ELAAS seemed reluctant to help, particularly over an error he discovered on a Judgement, where the Judge had not checked back on evidence.   He did not want to stay on the line with me during the case.

Legal Professionals Not Following Bar Directives

I experienced Barristers and Solicitor not adhering to Bar Council directive, to put law above client's interest. I only discovered this recently.

During 2017Tribunal with Judge Livesey, there was a point during pre hearing when Judge Livesey found something in the evidence that annoyed him. He said Stancliffe's name aloud. At the same time, I noticed Ms Palmer looking up shocked. Judge Livesey looked at me and said something to the effect I was genuine and praising me for the way I had presented myself. An autistic Mackenzie friend, in Court with me, also heard this. Shortly after, Judge Livesey picked up his papers and left, still angry at something. At the hearing, Ms Palmer had again blocked my giving evidence, but just before that I handed Judge a statement, including medical evidence from Dr van Driel of my autism diagnosis that AWP had blocked.

A FORMULA FOR CLOSURE

No doubt many people have views about the nature of closure. I am still not sure what this means in practical law, but AWP are miles from what I consider reasonable. In my view, this is a complete formula;

closure = 'telling your story' + apology + moral justice (investigation + financial recompense)

Investigation means *gaps in the employer's knowledge are filled, so errors do not re-occur.*

I hope this report leads to changes. There should not be a point when an employer or Tribunal closes its doors, because, as with Savile, dark deeds often go unreported for years.

Fair dealing: SUGGESTIONS FOR UPDATING systems

I would like to put this forward from the point of view of a victim. I have no technical or legal knowledge of HR or Tribunal systems but write from personal experience, finding current processes easily biased, highly stressful and often unfathomable.

Current Situation

HR systems, as evidenced by events at AWP, currently allow:

1. senior staff to refuse mediation even if this the policy of the organisation
2. biased investigations by staff connected to managers reported for bullying
3. no outside intervention or anyone to oversee procedures
4. vital bystanders refuse to come forward, thus giving bias to bully supports
5. victims forced into Dignity at Work investigations during trauma
6. HR failing to understand the longevity of trauma, depression and PTSD
7. when victims leave, it is easy for rogue staff to misrepresent victims
8. HR staff fail to understand or cope with the dynamics of bullying:
a. long-lasting nature of anger and frustration suffered by victims
b. bullying affects and reverses usual behaviour (personality changes)
c. fears of bystanders, e.g. loss of reputation, career, professional contacts
d. the extent to which professionals lie on behalf of colleagues
e. how easy it is to misperceive situations
f. overestimate the competence of investigating professionals - i.e. holding a profession or high office is not an indicator of a sound investigator

g. disbelief that professionals might sabotage an investigation

i. e.g. withholding or destruction of documents

h. no accountability for staff who tamper with investigations

i. no monitoring or accountability for bias or hidden agendas

Tribunals, evidenced by events at AWP, hold problems for victims:

1. when **ACAS refused** by employers, there is **no penalty**
   a. e.g. automatic judgement or judicial settlement
2. **preparation** is very difficult for stressed litigants-in-person:
   a. lack administrative support - obtaining documents, receipts, calls, as well as 'daily chores'
   b. lack funding e.g. paper, printing, telephone, postage, office time
   c. difficulty preparing documents in right format or formal language
   d. getting documents ready in limited time whilst traumatized
3. **very little legal support**, despite urban myths about such help
4. **'gamesmanship'** by legal professionals; abusing claimant's lack of sophistication:
   a. misleading claimants over preparation & content of bundles
   b. 'fudging' disclosure - e.g. delaying until the exact date, when claimants need more time to prepare
   c. trying to miss out vital documents by misleading claimant about bundle content or size
   d. putting fear in claimants about 'bankrupting' or 'punitive settlement' or expensive fees of barristers
5. **communication difficulties**, lack of understanding of nuances due to:
   a. differing social background or culture
   b. mental condition / sensory disorder where language / behaviour is easily misinterpreted
      e.g. Tourette's, autism, cerebral palsy

   c. victim fear: displayed through anger, non cooperation (a stance assumed to redress injured pride)
   d. 'invisible anxiety' e.g. claimant 'puts on front' to save humiliation of appearing weak
   e. Judge not looking at claimant does not perceive fear, masked by a 'brave front'
   f. silence of victim or lack of eye contact, e.g. in autism, misperceived as 'shifty', arrogance or 'cocky'

6. **difficulty understanding legal requirements**, despite Tribunal staff efforts;
   a.   explanatory leaflets far too long to take in during trauma
   b.   a single process explained through too many different channels, e.g. remission of fees requires visiting several web pages, is challenging in itself
   c.   lack of Court understanding of how little information can be taken in, by a victim in trauma
   d.   legalese - e.g. 'skeleton argument;' 'bundle content;' 'estoppel'
   e.   exasperated court staff - over busy because not enough staff
   f.   misunderstandings about which department deals with what
   g.   embarrassment of misunderstanding, leading to failure to ask, check or assumptions
7. **not allowed sufficient recovery time** before proceeding to Tribunal:
   a.   a year might seem a long time but is not, for someone in trauma
   b.   mental instability takes far longer to recover than is appreciated
   c.   claimant appears more stable than they are, when viewed through writing rather than in person
   d.   unable to make a coherent case, which might appear angry, blaming, incomprehensive, etc
8. **fear and insecurities inside Court room:**
   a.   these are often under estimated by court and admin staff
   b.   renders claimant unable to speak clearly and delays thinking process;
   c.   leading to misinterpretation e.g. claimant fear of looking stupid leading to 'odd' behaviour
   d.   abuse by legal professionals e.g. being handed documents outside hearing room
   e.   the formal atmosphere, intimidating titles and clothing
   f.   difficulties following procedure, when to speak, what to say
   g.   being interrupted by barristers – no time to explain situation
   h.   interruptions leading to nervousness and missing vital topics
   i. fear and embarrassment of asking for toilet or stress break
   j. warping of time during distress leads to disorientation

Discussion

Overall, my experience of court procedures was, that I wish I had never started. It was very stressful and appeared rushed, though looking back it took place over a considerable time. I was lucky at my last but one hearing to have a Mackenzie friend, also autistic, which felt better but nevertheless I was unable to speak extemporaneously because of my autism. When Judge got up to leave, I wanted to call him back, as I wanted to say more, but found myself unable to do so. Also, the solicitor Mr Gutteridge handing me a document just outside Court threw me. I did not know what to do with it. I was thinking of this all the way through the hearing. At the telephone hearing (*the case was in London, which for me would be like travelling to Australia also impossibly expensive*) I felt the same. I was not given time to say what I wanted, and in any case I really dislike the telephone but there was no other option. It all felt over in seconds, and that was my last chance at Justice.

I do not think other claimants in my situation will think, feel and act very differently to me. I hope this to be the value of this report. Court is like speaking the same language yet divided by meaning: *'The Etruscan inscriptions are written in Greek letters and can therefore be read, but the language is not understood."* [Derek Roe, Prehistory]. Employers want 'the problem dealt with' i.e. the fastest, cheapest solution with minimal bad press or internal disruption. Employers like AWP, despite claiming to care, do not care when there are broken cogs like bullying and victimization in their machine. Their continual refusal to hear me, claiming full settlement was made (when it was not), leaving me in dire straits with no closure, suffering over a decade, is inhuman and outrageous. So how to deal with such a seemingly impassable dichotomy?

Suggested Amendments to Legislation

HR Systems
1. HR staff undertake training including dynamics of bullying at work
2. potential victims offered immediate access to a confidential helpline
3. supportive counselling offered free, away from bully employer
4. no reporting of victims names to the employer
5. 'Dignity at Work' must be out-of-house - ACAS being first choice

Tribunal System

1. conduct all NHS bullying (Dignity at Work) investigations via ACAS, with interviews by ACAS staff
2. legislate for no 'Dignity at Work' investigations conducted in-house, unless by Tribunal-appointed professional mediators, to include Judicial Settlement
3. instead of Tribunals, have tribunal cases conducted through ACAS;
   a. (disables rogue seniors or HR and prevents NHS Trusts from abusing law to crush victims)
   b. employer must provide ACAS with full disclosure, with Directors signing legal agreement this has been provided
   c. ACAS provide a report to a Judge, using ACAS contracted legal professionals #
   d. cases decided by a Judge in chamber - alleviating need for victim to appear in Court room
   e. the same Judge, where possible, to oversee the whole case end to end (deep knowledge of case)
   f. judgement reported and explained to victim by ACAS mediator
4. if employer attempts to bypass ACAS system, immediate default Judicial Settlement
5. Legal funding removed from all NHS employers #
   a. redirected funding to ACAS to contract legal experts and more trained mediators
   b. (legal experts thus integrated into a solution, rather than a 'battle' with victim)
   c. where required, persons with high level diplomatic service experience, contracted to oversee difficult / enduring disputes
   d. integrate Union officials, e.g. potential 'Mackenzie friend' or to help with applications
   e. Union officials can report to ACAS breaches of employment law, obviating blaming of victims
6. Judicial Settlement, based on ACAS findings aided by legal professionals, is fair to both parties
7. 'Closure' legislated as including:
   a. full report by ACAS, agreed by parties, given claimant, employer; held permanently on Tribunal files
   b. where appropriate, full written apology to victim
   c. victim enabled to write to staff making allegations, refuting allegations. Copy to be kept at ACAS.

d. no withholding of full reference, where deemed appropriate by Tribunal
e. no interference by senior staff / HR with victim's potential new employer[s]   or work contracts
f. Tribunal overseeing investigation/ removal/ sanctions against senior staff who perpetrated bullying
g. damages/ reparation/ financial settlement by Judicial Settlement
i.   taking claimant to[at least] where they were, before employ at toxic firm
h. for any breach by employer, instant access for victim to Tribunal for rectification/sanctions

Other Agencies

1.   extend Whistleblower Law to cover staff-on-staff bullying
     a.   include provision for historic cases, over a period of time
2.   empower CQC to investigate staff on staff bullying - this DOES affect patient care
3.   complaints against members of organisations conducted by independent arbitrators
4.   give MP's greater powers for mediating on behalf of victims
5.   Union officials can be asked to represent victims, if victims wish this
6.   a permanent standing Committee run by Tribunal, to include all agencies connected with employment issues
7.   an enquiry into the nature of investigators like PALS:
     a.   appoint an Inspector
     b.   analyse their scope & where remit and parameters are duplicated
     c.   send in mystery shoppers to check their credibility
     d.   produce a list of charities funding agencies, including National Lottery
     e.   viability - reducing number of agencies, and/or improving   their connectivity - based on victim need
     f.   analyse and update terms of reference
     g.   produce new, integrative user literature, in Plain English
     h.   regular auditing (unplanned visits by inspector)
     i.   registration, with an annual audit of ALL agencies

APPENDIX ONE: CAST OF CHARACTERS -
worksites, addresses & contact details removed

NAME / TITLE
Veronica Barnes, Secretary to Dr Howells
Aleya Begum, Psychology Assistant
Anita Corfe, Senior Psychology Assistant
Marianne Richards, Counsellor
AWP MANAGEMENT
Dr Anne Booth, Senior Psychologist
Dr Elizabeth Howells, Psychologist, Manager
Dr William Jerrom, Head of Psychology
Gwyneth Knight, Assistant HR Manager
Annett e Law, Training & Supervision Mgr, Deputy to Dr Howells
Andrew Mitchell, HR Manager, Victoria Hosp
Dr Susan O'Connor, Medical Director
Christopher Stancliffe, Dignity Investigator
Barbara Stapleton, Counsellor, variously: Lead Clinician, Cluster lead, & Mentor to Marianne Richards
ELDENE SURGERY
Dr Eric Holiday, Lead GP
Mrs Christine Mott, Practice Mgr
AWP Legal Team
Rahim Amarshi, Assistant Solicitor
James Gutteridge, Solicitor
Anya Palmer, Barrister
Liam Stallard, AWP Paralegal
AUTISM EXPERTS
Tony Attwood, world autism expert
Simon Barron-Cohen, Autism expert Prof of Developmental Psychology
Dr van Driel, Consultant Psychiatrist
Dr Blackwell (retired)

OTHER ORGANISATIONS
Jo Collins, AWP PALS Manager
Val Jannsen, BANES Health Commissioner
George O'Neill, BANES Commissioner, Head of Mental Health
Petra Freeman, Whistleblower Guardian

Marianne Richards contacts:
Dr Blackwell
Dr Geary/ Dr Britten, current GP
Caroline Wiltshire, Counsellor, Westbury
Dr van Driel, Consultant Psychiatrist

APPENDIX TWO: regarding evidence documents

117 evidence documents, together with the report, are filed in the office of the Senior President of Tribunals, to whom the report was sent in January 2020. A copy of the report is currently with 'NHS England and NHS Improvement' (both agencies being incorporated). The author has 1047 documents on a searchable database, of which a good proportion were withheld, when they should have been provided for Tribunals. AWP solicitors, Bevan Britten, colluded in this.

The author agrees to make available [to bone fide agencies only] copies of documents referred to in this report. Examples of bone fide agencies:

- NHS England and NHS Improvement
- Investigators from CQC
- Senior members of bone fide organisations such as BPS, BACP
- Investigative Journalists with press passes
- Social researchers from any major University, in the UK or elsewhere
- MP members of relevant all-party committees
- Senior members of the Judiciary or judicial committees
- Researchers working on behalf of the TUC
- Representatives from anti bullying at work organisations

MISSING DOCUMENTS

- Dr Anne Booth's 'final Dignity Report'
- Dr Bill Jerrom/ Abigail Moore - Disciplinary Report - never disclosed
- doc G point 6: Stancliffe to Jerrom
- 2017 'Metherall Report' - never took place though frequently referred to

ULYSSES
[extract]

'Tis not too late to seek a newer world.
Push off and sitting well in order smite
The sounding furrows; for my purpose holds
To sail beyond the sunset, and the baths
Of all the western stars, until I die.
It may be that the gulfs will wash us down:
It may be we shall touch the Happy Isles
And see the great Achilles, whom we knew.

Tho' much is taken, much abides; and though
We are not now that strength which in old days
Moved earth & heaven
That which we are, we are;
One equal temper of heroic hearts,
Made weak by time and fate but strong in will
To strive, to seek, to find and not to yield.

Printed in Great Britain
by Amazon